KEY A1

STARTER

Von Jon Wright

Beratende Mitarbeit
Dietlind Unger, Leipzig

Cornelsen

KEY A1 Starter
Im Auftrag des Verlages erarbeitet von Dr. Jon Wright, Manchester

mit Beiträgen von
Lisa Lubin, Mark Wolters

Grammatikanhang
Dr. Lars-Georg Wigger, Reutlingen

Wortlisten
Oliver Busch, Berlin

Beratende Mitarbeit
Dietlind Unger, Leipzig

Redaktion
Martin Maier

Redaktionelle Mitarbeit
Zsusza Parádi (Phonetik), Dietlind Unger, Katrina Walsh, Martin Walsh

Bildredaktion
Uta Hübner

Projektleitung
Murdo MacPhail

Gesamtgestaltung und technische Umsetzung
Klein & Halm Grafikdesign, Berlin

Illustration
Chetan Kumar, London S. 18, 29
Bettina Kumpe, Braunschweig innere Umschlagseite vorne, S. 7, 13, 21, 22, 24, 25, 27, 31, 35, 37, 39, 40, 41, 42
Frank Maier, Stuttgart S. 46

www.cornelsen.de

1. Auflage, 1. Druck 2011

Alle Drucke dieser Auflage sind inhaltlich unverändert
und können im Unterricht nebeneinander verwendet werden.

Druck: CS-Druck CornelsenStürtz, Berlin

ISBN 978-3-06-20812-8

Inhalt gedruckt auf säurefreiem Papier aus nachhaltiger Forstwirtschaft.

Welcome to KEY!

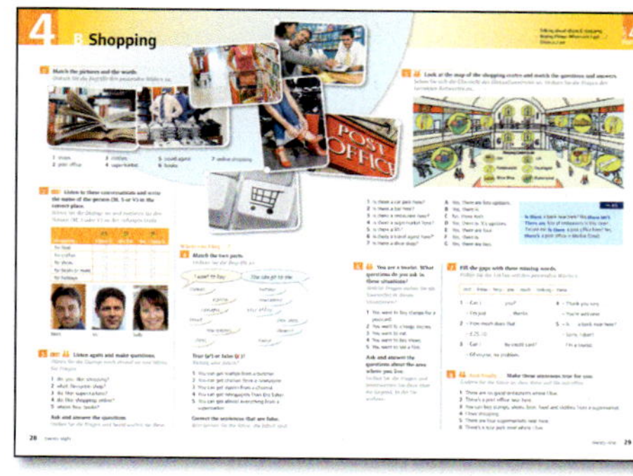

Alles in **KEY** ist darauf ausgerichtet, Sie dabei zu unterstützen, in einem angemessenen Lerntempo und mit Spaß Englisch zu lernen, um die englische Sprache sicher anwenden zu können. Der **KEY Starter A1** führt in kleinen Schritten an die ersten Bausteine und Strukturen der englischen Sprache heran und gibt Ihnen langsam Sicherheit, sich in der englischen Sprache zurechtzufinden. Besonderes Augenmerk haben wir dabei auf vielseitige und interessante Themen, vor allem aber auf natürliche Alltagssprache gelegt.

Jede Doppelseite ist für ca. 90 Minuten konzipiert und bietet abwechslungsreiche Aktivitäten zu einem thematischen Schwerpunkt. Die verschiedenen Sprechanlässe und Übungen sind dem realistischen Alltag entnommen. Sie behandeln wesentliche Strukturen, wichtigen Wortschatz und vor allem praktische Ausdrücke und Wendungen, die Sie sofort anwenden können.

KEY: Ihr Schlüssel zur englischen Sprache!

Jede der sechs *Units* im **KEY Starter A1** besteht aus drei Doppelseiten (*Parts* A, B und C). In den *Parts* A und B jeder *Unit* werden die Grundlagen für die neuen Strukturen gelegt. *Part C* (*Homestudy*) ist in erster Linie für das Selbststudium und als Nachbereitung der Unit gedacht.

In der Abschluss-*Unit 6* wiederholen und festigen Sie bereits erlernte Strukturen.

Die **KEY** Journals sind ein ganz besonderer Bestandteil. Auf diesen Seiten haben wir für Sie interessante und unterhaltsame kurze Texte und Bilder ausgewählt. Die Journals können in den Unterricht integriert werden, animieren aber gleichzeitig zum Weiterlesen außerhalb des Kursraumes.

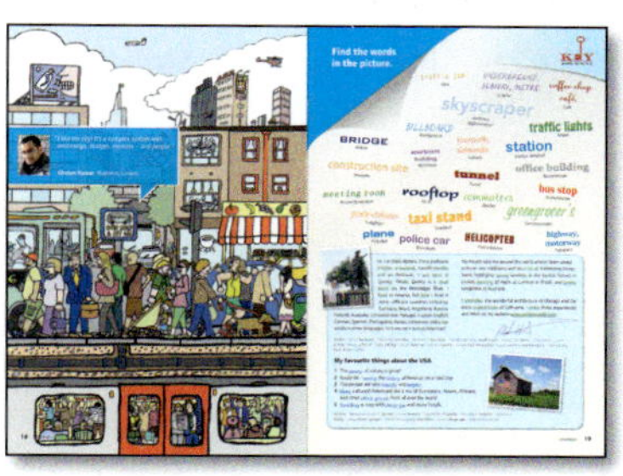

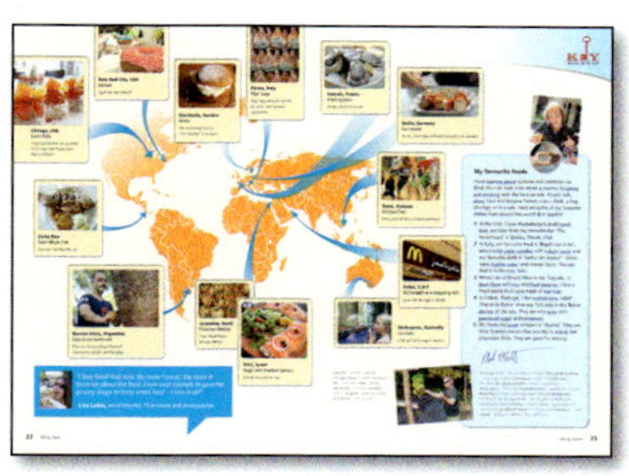

Stöbern Sie einfach einmal auf diesen Seiten und Sie werden schnell merken, dass Sie schon sehr schnell viel mehr verstehen, als Sie vielleicht am Anfang gedacht haben.

Außerdem im **KEY Starter A1**:

- Chronologische und alphabetische **Wortlisten** mit allen Vokabeln, Lautschrift und Übersetzungen im Anhang.
- Auf der **Audio-CDs** sind alle Hörtexte der *Units* zusammengestellt.
- Sämtliche **Arbeitsanweisungen mit deutscher Übersetzung** darunter.
- Auf der inneren Umschlagseite finden Sie zusätzlich schnell die wesentlichen Begriffe und Wendungen, die in den Aufgabenstellungen verwendet werden.

Viel Erfolg und Spaß mit KEY wünscht Ihnen Ihr Cornelsen-Team

Table of contents

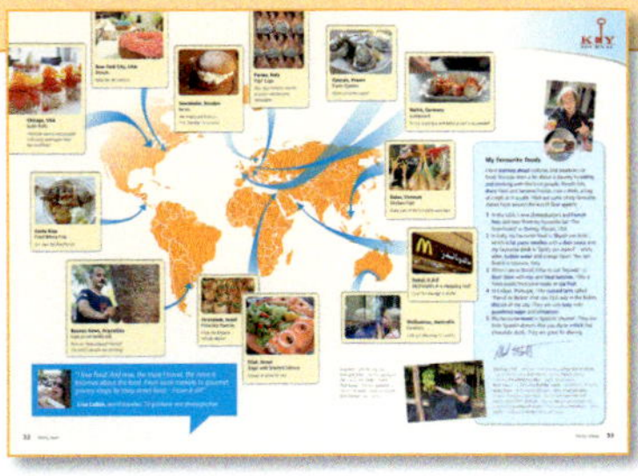

public transport
Transport tips

1 A Hello, I'm …

1 **English or not?**
Englisch oder nicht?

JAMBO Salut
Kia ora Hello
Hi Ciao How are you?
Ahoj Guten Morgen
Bonjour ¿Qué tal?

2 **Match the English words to the pictures.**
Ordnen Sie die englischen Begriffe den passenden Bildern zu.

chocolate • tea • coffee • wine • beer • house • music • garden • pizza • water • taxi

1.2 **Listen and repeat.**
Hören Sie zu und sprechen Sie nach.

Hello, I'm …

3 1.3 **Read and listen.**
Lesen Sie und hören Sie zu.

Repeat with your names.
Wiederholen Sie den Dialog und setzen Sie Ihre Namen ein.

How many classmates can you say hello to in one minute?
Wie viele andere Kursteilnehmer können Sie in einer Minute begrüßen?

Yes or no?

4 1.4 **Listen and tick (✔) the words you hear.**
Hören Sie zu und haken Sie die Wörter ab, die erwähnt werden.

apple	pizza
beer	place
car	spaghetti
chocolate	tea
coffee	water
fruit	whisky
pasta	wine

I'm … and this is …

5 1.5 **Listen and practise this dialogue.**
Hören Sie zu und üben Sie diesen Dialog.

Jane	Hello.
Max	Hi. I'm Max.
Jane	Hi. Nice to meet you. I'm Jane.
Max	Hi. And this is Fran.
Jane	Hi Fran.
Fran	Hello. Nice to meet you, Jane.
Jane	Pete – Max and Fran.
Pete	Hi Max.
Max	Hi Pete. This is Fran.
Fran	Hello. Nice to meet you.
Pete	Nice to meet you, too.

Practise this dialogue with your names.
Üben Sie den Dialog mit Ihren Namen.

A Hi, I'm …
B Hi. I'm … Nice to meet you.
A Nice to meet you, too. This is …
C Hi. Nice to meet you.

6 **Make four sentences.**
Bilden Sie vier Sätze.

not = *nicht*

1 I'm	**A** 's Bill.
2 My name	**B** meet you.
3 Nice to	**C** is Fran.
4 This	**D** not Jane.

This is my …

7 **Make sentences with the words.**
Bilden Sie Sätze mit diesen Wörtern.

party pen car place

This is my …

class garden chair house book

8 **Make three sentences about you.**
Bilden Sie drei Sätze über sich.

1 I'm ………………………………………………………….
2 I'm not ………………………………………………….
3 This is my ……………………………………………….

9 And finally … **English or not?**
Englisch oder nicht?

ADIOS See you Kwaheri Goodbye Bye Ciao Tot ziens Ahoj Take care Aroha nui

Max Good party, thanks, Pete.
Pete OK. Goodbye, Max.
Max Goodbye.

1 B Are you from …?

1 **Call out the name of one student. When you hear your name, answer and show one object you have with you. Then call out another name.**
Sagen Sie den Namen eines anderen Teilnehmers. Wenn Sie Ihren Namen hören, antworten Sie und zeigen Sie einen Gegenstand, den Sie bei sich haben. Rufen Sie dann einen anderen Kursteilnehmer auf.

Peter?
Yes, I'm here, and this is my pen. Jack?

Tell your partner three things about you.
Erzählen Sie Ihrem Partner drei Dinge über sich.

I'm …

… and this is my …

1. I am …
2. This is …
3. …

2 1.6 **Listen. Who is in the car hire office?**
Hören Sie den Dialog an. Wer ist in dem Büro der Autovermietung?

☐ Ms Sarah Smith ☐ Ms Sarah Jackson
☐ Ms Sarah Birmingham

→ 49
I **am** / **'m** Peter. I'm Peter.
You **are** / **'re** Sarah. You're Sarah.

Are you …?

3 1.7 **Listen and complete the form.**
Hören Sie den Dialog an und ergänzen Sie das Formular.

CAR HIRE FORM	
Family name:	Smith
First name:	D
City:	
Car:	BMW

KEEP A COPY FOR YOUR RECORDS

– Hello.
– How can I help you?
– I'm here for my BMW.
– OK. What's your name?
– Smith. Mr Smith.
– Are you Mr D. Smith?
– Yes.
– Here you are. Mr David Smith from Liverpool.
– No, I'm Dennis, not David. And I'm not from Liverpool.
– Oh. You're Dennis. Are you from Manchester?
– Yes, I'm from Manchester.
– OK. Yes.

→ 49
Are you Harry?
Are you from here? Yes, I **am**.
Are you from Liverpool? No, I'**m not**.
Are you English?

What's your answer?
Und wie lautet Ihre Antwort?

I'm from …

4 **Complete the table with these words.**
Vervollständigen Sie die Tabelle mit den folgenden Begriffen.

Spain • Bulgaria • German • English • Croatian • American • French • Italy • Polish • Switzerland

I'm from … / I'm …

Country	Nationality
England	
France	
	Spanish
Germany	
	Italian
Poland	
America / The United States	
	Swiss
Croatia	
	Bulgarian

5 **Ask and answer these questions.**
Stellen Sie Ihrem Partner Fragen und beantworten diese.

1 - Are you from Spain?
 - ……………………………………

2 - Are you American?
 - …………………………………….

3 - Are you from Paris?
 - …………………………………….

Are you from …?

Yes, I am. I'm English.

No, I'm not. I'm not English. I'm from …

And you?
Are you from …?

6 1.8 **Listen and write down the letters you hear.**
Hören Sie zu und notieren Sie die Buchstaben, die Sie hören.

A_1 B_3 C_3 D_2 E_1 F_4 G_2 H_4 I_1 J_8
K_5 L_1 M_3 N_1 O_1 P_3 Q_{10} R_1 S_1 T_1
U_1 V_4 W_4 X_8 Y_4 Z_{10}

Which words do you hear?
Welche Wörter hören Sie?

7 And finally … **Spell the following words to a partner.**
Buchstabieren Sie Ihrem Partner die folgenden Begriffe.

1 Your family name: ……………………………
2 The name of your street: ……………………………
3 The name of your favourite city: ……………………………
4 The name of a country: ……………………………
5 A word from this lesson in English: ……………………………

1 C Homestudy

1 Complete the cards.

Vervollständigen Sie die Karten.

1

My name is Cleopatra
I'm from Egypt
I am Egyptian

2

My name is Till Eulenspiegel
I'm from ...
I am ...

3

My name is Genghis Khan
I'm from Mongolia
I am ...

4

My name is Robin Hood
I'm from ...
I am ...

2 Which country is wrong?

Welches Land passt nicht?

Continent	Country		
1 Europe	France	England	~~Japan~~
2 Africa	South Africa	Tunisia	New Zealand
3 Asia	Thailand	India	Spain
4 North America	Canada	Colombia	The United States
5 South America	Argentina	Brazil	Morocco
6 Australasia	Australia	Samoa	Peru

3 Complete the sentences with the "wrong" countries from 2.

Vervollständigen Sie die Sätze mit den „falschen" Ländern aus Aufgabe 2.

1 Japan is not in Europe.
It's in Asia.

2 ... is in ... .
It's not in Africa.

3 ... is not in Asia.
It's in ... .

4 ... is not in North America.
It's in ... .

5 ... is not in South America.
It's in ... .

6 ... is not in Australasia.
It's in ... .

4 1.9 Listen to the sentences. Who is the speaker?

Hören Sie zu und entscheiden Sie, welche Person gerade spricht.

1 ☐ Hitomi Kitano ☐ Maria Varese
2 ☐ Mauro Varese ☐ Larry Lewis
3 ☐ Monika Czarnok ☐ Hitomi Kitano
4 ☐ Urs Müller ☐ Mauro Varese
5 ☐ Maria Varese ☐ Hitomi Kitano
6 ☐ Urs Müller ☐ Larry Lewis

Name: Kitano
First name: Hitomi
Nationality: Japanese

Name: Müller
First name: Urs
Nationality: Swiss

Name: Czarnok
First name: Monika
Nationality: American

Name: Varese
First name: Mauro
Nationality: Italian

Name: Lewis
First name: Larry
Nationality: American

Name: Varese
First name: Maria
Nationality: Italian

5

My name is Sitting Bull
I'm from ...
I am ...

6

My name is Buddha
I'm from ...
I am ...

7

My name is The Little Mermaid
I'm from ...
I am ...

8

My name is William Tell
I'm from ...
I am ...

5 Match the questions and answers.

Ordnen Sie die Fragen und Antworten zu.

1 Are you English?
2 Are you from China?
3 I'm from Spain. And you?
4 Are you from Germany?
5 Are you from Italy?

A No, I'm not Chinese. I'm from Japan.
B Yes, I'm Italian.
C I'm from Berlin.
D No, I'm not from Germany. I'm Swiss.
E Yes, my name's Jon.

6 Unscramble the words.

Entknoten Sie die Buchstaben.

1 This is my FEDRIN, Jane.
...
2 I'm a student. This is my SCALS.
...
3 Nice to ETME you.
...
4 This is my SEOHU.
...
5 I'm Jean, from RACFEN.
...

7 Find all the words.

Finden Sie alle Wörter in dem Kreuzworträtsel.

ACROSS →:
4 *Schokolade, Praline*
6 *Haus*
8 *Pizza*
10 *Taxi*
11 *Bier*

DOWN ↓:
1 *Kaffee*
2 *Garten*
3 *Tee*
5 *Musik*
7 *Wasser*
9 *Wein*

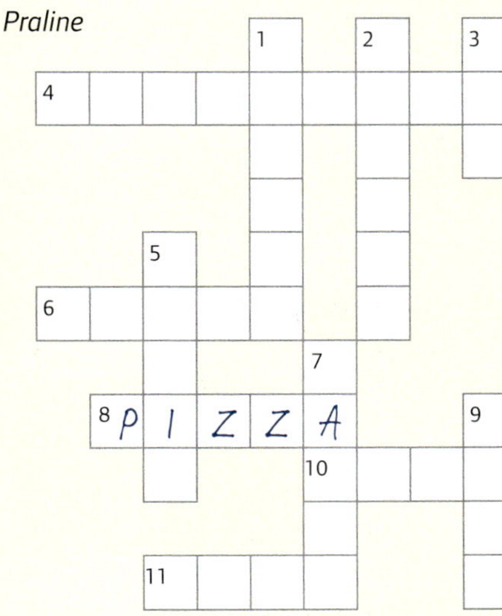

Key classroom language

- Work in pairs.
- I understand.
- Write the answer.
- Open your books.
- Listen.
- Please repeat.
- Sorry?
- That's right.
- Again, please.

2 A And your number?

1 Choose a city and ask questions to find the city.
Wählen Sie eine Stadt aus und stellen Sie Fragen, um die Stadt zu finden.

Paris Rome Sydney
Moscow Washington D.C.
Berlin London New York
Madrid Lisbon

☐ Colosseum ☐ Eiffel Tower
☐ Red Square ☐ Sydney Opera House ☐ White House

Is it in Europe?
Yes, it is.
Is it a German city?
No, it isn't.
Is it Paris?
Yes, it is.

2 Match the words and numbers.
Ordnen Sie die ausgeschriebenen Zahlen den Ziffern zu.

☐ two ☐ eight ☐ five ☐ six ☐ ten ☐ one
☐ three ☐ four ☐ nine ☐ seven

Alphabet & numbers

3 1.10 Listen carefully. Which of these number plates do you hear?
Hören Sie genau hin – welche Nummernschilder hören Sie?

Read out the number plates.
Lesen Sie die Nummernschilder laut vor.

What's your number?

4 1.11 Listen and write the phone number for each person.
Hören Sie und notieren Sie die Telefonnummern.

Jane: ....

Simon: ....

Telephone numbers
0161 = oh-one-six-one
5522 = five-five-two-two = double-five, double-two

Counting numbers
0, 1, 2, 3 = zero, one, two, three

Places in a city

5 **Look at the pictures and complete the sentences.**
Sehen Sie sich die Bilder an und vervollständigen Sie die Sätze.

1 cinema | school.
2 restaurant | hotel.
3 restaurant | pub.
4 theatre | cathedral.
5 street | hotel.
6 museum | school.
7 cathedral | pub.
8 pub | cinema.
9 museum | street.

→ 49

Yes, it **is** a hotel. It**'s** a hotel in Paris. No, it **is not** a cinema.
It**'s not** in London. No, it **isn't** a cinema.

6 **Make six short dialogues.**
Bilden Sie sechs kurze Dialoge.

Is St Paul's a theatre? Is it a pub? Is the Louvre a school? Is the Odeon a hotel? Is the Ritz a restaurant? Is … a …?	No, it isn't. Yes, it is.	It's a cathedral. It's a cinema. It's a museum. It's a motel.

→ 50

a museum, **a** cinema, **a** restaurant
the Louvre, **the** Eiffel Tower, **the** Ritz

7 **Match the questions and answers.**
Verbinden Sie die Fragen mit den passenden Antworten.

1 What's your name?
2 What's that?
3 What's 'Kino' in English?
4 What's your number?
5 What's your address?

A It's 07971 824955.
B It's 5 Market Street.
C It's cinema.
D It's my mobile.
E Michael.

Ask your partner four questions.
Stellen Sie Ihrem Partner vier Fragen.

8 **And finally … Complete the list. Then ask two students. Write the answers.**
Vervollständigen Sie die Liste. Fragen Sie dann zwei Kursteilnehmer und notieren Sie deren Antworten.

What's your phone number?
It's …

B No, this is a museum

1 Write the missing numbers.
Ergänzen Sie die fehlenden Zahlen.

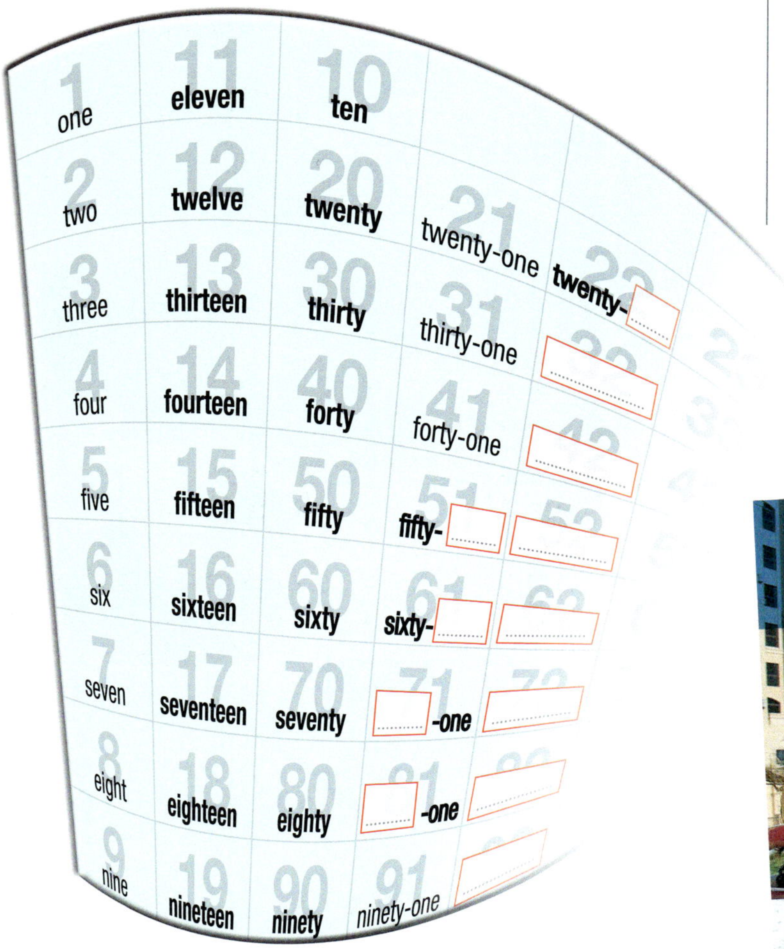

2 1.12 Listen and write the numbers you hear.
Hören Sie zu und notieren Sie die Ziffern, die Sie hören.

nineteen eleven thirty-four

twenty fifty-eight eighty-five

twelve forty-five ninety-nine

1 ....

2 ....

3 ....

4 ....

Which numbers are missing?
Welche Zahlen wurden nicht genannt?

3 Say these sentences.
Sagen Sie diese Sätze.

1 It's 1987.
2 I was born in 1963.
3 It's 11.35 now.
4 My favourite number is 33.
5 My house is number 17.

Give your real answers.
Setzen Sie Ihre eigenen Angaben in die Sätze ein.

4 1.13 Listen. Which is the right city tour?
Hören Sie zu – welche Tour hören Sie?

A–Z Tour

10.30	Visit the City Museum (30 minutes)
11.15	Visit the cathedral of Saint John (20 minutes)
11.45	Visit Market Street shops (one hour)
1.10 – 2.00	Restaurant
2.20	Visit the theatre

City Tour

10.30	Visit the cathedral of Saint John. (20 minutes)
11.20	Visit the City Museum (40 minutes)
12.30	Visit the theatre (30 minutes)
1.10 – 2.00	Restaurant
2.30	Visit Market Street (one hour)

5 Match the questions and answers.

Ordnen Sie die Fragen den passenden Antworten zu.

1 It's 12.40. Where's Bill?
2 It's 11.30. Where's Angela?
3 It's 2.00. Where's Daisy?
4 It's 10.30. Where's Angela?
5 It's 1.50. Where's Bill?

A She's in the restaurant.
B He's in the theatre.
C She's in the cathedral.
D She's in the museum.
E He's in the restaurant.

Choose a different time and ask a question.
Wählen Sie eine andere Zeit und fragen Sie Ihren Partner.

→ 49

Angela **is** in the restaurant at 1.10, and she **is** in the theatre at 2.20.

Bill **is** in the museum at 11.20, and he **is** in Market Street at 2.30.

Bill and Daisy **are** in the cathedral at 10.30, and they **are** in the museum at 11.20.

They **aren't** in the restaurant.

6 Match the questions and answers.

Ordnen Sie die Fragen den Antworten zu.

1 It's 10.45. Is Daisy in the cathedral?
2 It's 12.30. Is Angela in the theatre?
3 It's 2.40. Is Bill in Market Street?
4 It's 12.15. Is Bill in the restaurant?
5 It's 1.30. Are Daisy and Angela in the restaurant?
6 It's 11.10. Are Bill and Angela in the museum?

A No, he isn't.
B Yes, they are.
C Yes, she is.
D No, they aren't.
E Yes, he is.
F No, she isn't.

7 True (✔) or false (✘)?

Richtig oder falsch?

1 This is Daisy. She's 39.
2 She's Scottish.
3 She isn't from Edinburgh. She's from Glasgow.
4 She's a teacher.
5 Daisy and Angela are friends.

8 And finally … Introduce a person to the class.

Stellen Sie dem Kurs eine Person vor.

2 C Homestudy

1 **Match the pictures to the words in the box and make sentences.**
Ordnen Sie die Bilder den Begriffen zu und bilden Sie Sätze.

boarding card • café • car park • lounge • ~~plane~~ • restaurant

1 *It's a plane* ....
2 ....
3 ....
4 ....
5 ....
6 ....

2 1.14 **Look at the boarding card. Listen to the dialogue and correct the mistakes.**
Sehen Sie sich die Bordkarte an. Hören Sie den Dialog und korrigieren Sie die Fehler.

3 **Choose the the right verb form.**
Wählen Sie die richtige Verbform aus.

1 Angela and Bill ~~is~~ | (are) at the airport.
2 Angela and Bill is | are friends.
3 Munich is | isn't the destination.
4 The gate number on the boarding card is | are right.
5 Munich is | isn't in Switzerland.
6 The departure time and seat number is | are wrong.
7 Bill and Angela are | aren't German.
8 Angela's name is | isn't Schmidt.

4 Complete the answers.
Vervollständigen Sie die Sätze.

1 – Is Angela in Munich?
– Yes, she *is* .
2 – Is Big Ben in Munich?
– No, it isn't. It's ....
3 – Is the boarding card wrong?
– Yes, ...
4 – Are Glasgow and Edinburgh in England?
– No, ...
5 – Are Bill and Angela friends?
– Yes, ...

5 Match the questions and answers.
Ordnen Sie die Fragen und Antworten zu.

1 Where's Notre Dame?	A It's in London.
2 Where's the Red Square?	B It's in Milan.
3 Where's the British Museum?	C It's in Moscow.
4 Where's the White House?	D It's in Paris.
5 Where's La Scala?	E It's in Washington.

6 Complete the questions.
Ergänzen Sie die Fragen.

1 Where | Disneyland?
Where is Disneyland? ?
2 Where | the Eiffel Tower?
.... ?
3 Where | the Red Square?
.... ?
4 Where | the 'Reichstag'?
.... ?
5 Where | the Golden Gate Bridge?
.... ?

7 Now answer the questions.
Beantworten Sie nun die Fragen.

1 *Disneyland is in ...* .
2 ....
3 ....
4 ....
5 ....

8 Fill in the gaps with *a* or *the*.
Setzen Sie ,a' oder ,the' in die Lücken ein.

1 Notre Dame is *a* cathedral.
2 London is .... city in England. It's .... capital of England.
3 My car is in .... car park here.
4 Bill isn't .... German name.
5 La Scala isn't .... cinema. It's .... name of the Opera House in Milan.
6 My name is Angelique. It's .... French name.

9 What's the missing number in each line?
Welche Zahlen fehlen hier?

1 52 11 43 96
fifty-two, forty-three, ninety-six *eleven*
2 13 33 28 82
thirteen, thirty-three, eighty-two ....
3 7 17 70 72
seven, seventy, seventy-two ....

10 Write the missing number.
Schreiben Sie die fehlende Zahl.

1	10	20	.....	40	50	*thirty*
2	10	.....	20	25	30	....
3	.....	14	15	16	17	....
4	42	53	64	75	.....	....
5	97	96	95	.....	93	....

Key classroom language

- Hello again.
- What's the answer?
- What's ... in English?
- That's right.
- I see.
- Well done.
- How do you spell ...?
- How do you say ... in English?
- That's not right. It's wrong.
- Very good!

"I like my city! It's a complex system with motorways, bridges, markets – and people."

Chetan Kumar, illustrator, London

KEY JOURNAL

Find the words in the picture.

traffic jam
Stau

UNDERGROUND, SUBWAY, METRO
U-Bahn

coffee shop café,
Café

skyscraper
Hochhaus, Wolkenkratzer

BILLBOARD
Werbeplakat

traffic lights
Ampel

BRIDGE
Brücke

footpath, sidewalk
Fußweg

station
Station, Bahnhof

apartment building
Wohnhaus

construction site
Baustelle

office building
Bürogebäude

tunnel
Tunnel

bus stop
Bushaltestelle

meeting room
Besprechungsraum

rooftop
Dach

commuters
Pendler

greengrocer's
Gemüsehändler

pedestrians
Fußgänger

taxi stand
Taxistand

plane
Flugzeug

police car
Polizeiauto

HELICOPTER
Hubschrauber

highway, motorway
Autobahn

Hi, I'm Mark Wolters. I'm a professor, a father, a husband, a world traveller and an American. I was born in Quincy, Illinois. Quincy is a small town on the Mississippi River. I lived in America, but later I lived in many different countries including: Germany, Brazil, Argentina, Austria, Finland, Australia, Lithuania and Portugal. I speak English, German, Spanish, Portuguese, Italian, Lithuanian and a few words in other languages, so I am not a typical American!

My travels take me around the world where I learn about cultures and traditions and do a lot of interesting things. Some highlights: eating sardines at the Santos festival in Lisbon, dancing all night at Carnival in Brazil, and seeing kangaroos in Australia.

I remember the wonderful architecture of Chicago and the crazy superstitions of Lithuania. I share these experiences and more on my website www.woltersworld.com.

father – Vater; **husband** – Ehemann; **traveller** – Reisender; **was born** – (wurde) geboren; **small town** – kleiner Ort; **lived** – lebte; **later** – später; **a few** – einige; **a lot of** – viele; **eating** – essen; **dancing** – tanzen; **seeing** – sehen; **(to) remember** – (sich) erinnern; **superstitions** – Aberglaube; **(to) share** – teilen

My favourite things about the USA

1 The variety of nature is great!
2 Route 66 - seeing the history of America on a road trip.
3 The people are very friendly and helpful.
4 Many cultures! Americans are a mix of Europeans, Asians, Africans, and other ethnic groups from all over the world.
5 Travelling is easy with cheap gas and many hotels.

variety – Vielfalt; **seeing** – sehen; **history** – Geschichte; **friendly** – freundlich; **helpful** – hilfsbereit; **many** – viele; **ethnic groups** – ethnische Gruppen; **travelling** – Reisen; **cheap gas** – preiswertes Benzin

3 A I like it!

1 **Read about Mark and what he likes or doesn't like.**
Lesen Sie, was Mark mag oder nicht mag.

I like football.

I don't like tennis.

Mark

Add Friend

Activities & interests

Sports	tennis, football, cricket, rugby, hockey
Music	classical music, rock music, jazz
Food & drink	tea, coffee, wine, beer, mineral water, spaghetti, fish
Other	summer, winter

2 **Are these sentences about Mark true (✔) or false (✘)?**
Sind diese Sätze über Mark richtig oder falsch?

1. I like coffee.
2. I don't like summer.
3. I like winter.
4. I like rock music.
5. I don't like classical music.
6. I like jazz music.

Correct the sentences that are wrong.
Korrigieren Sie die Sätze, die falsch sind.

3 **Now write five true sentences about you.**
Bilden Sie fünf Sätze über sich.

1 I like ....
2 I don't like ....
3 .... coffee.
4 .... jazz music.
5 .... football.

4 **Match the activities to the pictures.**
Ordnen Sie die Aktivitäten den Bildern zu.

watch TV • read a book • read a newspaper • listen to music • play football • go to the cinema • have a shower • phone a friend • use a computer • have a drink in the pub

5 1.15 Listen and put Mark's activities under the right picture.

Hören Sie zu und ordnen Sie Marks Aktivitäten den richtigen Bildern zu.

in the morning

I have a shower. ....

....

....

in the afternoon

....

....

....

in the evening

....

....

....

6 Complete these sentences about your day.

Ergänzen Sie die Sätze über Ihren eigenen Tagesablauf.

1 I .... in the morning.

2 I .... in the afternoon.

3 I don't .... in the afternoon.

4 I don't .... in the evening.

7 Highlight the plurals in these sentences.

Markieren Sie die Mehrzahlformen in den Sätzen.

1 I have a boy – Matteo. He's eight. My friend Sally has two girls.
2 I go to the cinema with Sue and Mark. They are my friends. They like horror films.
3 I have a computer but I don't play computer games. I send emails to friends.
4 My friend Bob likes cars. He has three.
5 I like sport. I play tennis and football, and I watch sport on TV.
6 In my class, five students have mobile phones and three have laptops.

→ 51

I have **two** car**s**, a BMW and a VW.
I speak **three** language**s**: English, French and German.
I work **eight** hour**s** a day.

Change the sentences so they are true for you.

Ändern Sie die Sätze so, dass diese auf Sie zutreffen.

8 And finally … How many true sentences can you make in two minutes?

Wie viele korrekte Sätze über sich können Sie in zwei Minuten bilden?

I	(don't)	live work use watch have read like listen to play go to	in a house in the city a computer TV a shower a newspaper tea music football work the cinema computer games three children	in Munich. in the evening. in the morning. in the afternoon. in Germany.

3 B Can you drive?

1 **Match the pictures and the activities.**
Verbinden Sie die Begriffe mit den passenden Bildern.

drive a car • cook a meal • play the piano • read a book • run a marathon

2 **Do you agree or not?**
Stimmen Sie zu oder nicht?

I agree. *I disagree.*

1 It's impossible to run a marathon in four hours.
2 It's possible to read a book in a day.
3 It's possible to play the piano when you are two.
4 It's impossible to read a book when you are one.
5 It's possible to cook a meal in five minutes.

3 **Match the questions and answers.**
Ordnen Sie die Fragen und Antworten zu.

1 Can you drive?
2 Can you speak Japanese?
3 Can you tell me the time?
4 Can you cook?
5 Can you speak English?

A Yes, I can. Pizza and toast!
B Yes, I can. I have a BMW.
C No, I can't.
D Yes, I can a little. Hello, how are you?
E Yes, it's 10.30.

→ 50
I **can** ski. It's easy. **Can** you?
Can you speak Japanese? No, I **can't**.

Ask and answer the questions.
Stellen Sie einander die Fragen und beantworten Sie diese.

4 **In the class, who can …**
Wer in diesem Kurs kann …

1 count to 20 in English?
2 name the capital of Mongolia?
3 play the piano?
4 remember the words from the last lesson?
5 name five famous English people?

5 **Answer the questions.**
Beantworten Sie die Fragen.

Yes, I do.
No, I don't

1 Do you live in Germany?
2 Do you like punk?
3 Do you live in a house?
4 Do you have a car?
5 Do you have a computer?

→ 49
Do you like classical music? No, **I don't**.
Do you live in Germany? Yes, **I do**.

6 Ask your partner three questions.

Stellen Sie Ihrem Partner drei Fragen.

1 Do you …

2 Do you …

3 Do you …

7 Complete the questions and answers.

Vervollständigen Sie die Fragen und Antworten.

do • don't • have • live

1 Do you .... a mobile? Yes, I do.

2 Do you like music? Yes, I ....

3 Do you work in the city? No, I ....

4 Do you .... a car? No, I don't.

5 Do you live in a house? No, I .... in a flat.

8 Look at Ken's diary and make sentences.

Sehen Sie sich Kens Terminkalender an und bilden Sie Sätze.

Monday	tennis in the evening
Tuesday	cinema with Jane
Wednesday	restaurant with Mike and Sue
Thursday	English class
Friday	football
Saturday	relax!
Sunday	

On Tuesday On Wednesday On Thursday On Friday On Saturday	Ken	goes has plays relaxes.	football. his English class. to the restaurant. to the theatre. to the cinema.

→ 49

Angela **reads** a book.
Jon **plays** tennis.
Ken **goes** to work.

9 1.16 Listen to the conversation. Who …

Hören Sie das Gespräch an. Wer …

	Bob (1)	John (2)
1 likes sport?	☐	☐
2 likes rugby?	☐	☐
3 likes football?	☐	☐
4 watches sport?	☐	☐
5 likes beer?	☐	☐
6 swims a little?	☐	☐
7 can't swim?	☐	☐
8 can speak a little Spanish?	☐	☐

10 And finally … Make these sentences true for you.

Ändern Sie die Sätze so, dass diese auf Sie zutreffen.

1 I can't cook.
2 I live in a house in London.
3 Today is Saturday.
4 I play football on Sunday.
5 I don't have a computer.

3 C Homestudy

1 **Unscramble the coloured words.**
Entknoten Sie die Buchstaben in den farbigen Wörtern.

1 In the morning, f e c e f o is great. I like it a lot. I don't like a e t.
....

2 My favourite drink? I like e r e b but I don't like n i w e.
....

3 Sports? Well, I don't like o f o t l a b l but I like e n t n s i.
....

2 **Complete the sentences with these words.**
Ergänzen Sie die Sätze mit diesen Wörtern.

play • watch • phone • read • have • listen

1 I .... TV in the evening
2 I can't .... books in Japanese.
3 I don't .... to classical music. I don't like it.
4 I .... football on Saturday.
5 I .... a shower in the morning.
6 I .... a friend in the evening.

3 **Change what Sheila and Paul say.**
Ändern Sie die Aussagen, die Sheila und Paul machen.

Sheila says she …
1 goes to work in the morning....................
2 ....
3 ....

Paul says he …
4 ....
5 ....
6 ....

4 **Complete the sentences with the right form of these words.**
Vervollständigen Sie die Sätze mit der passenden Form dieser Begriffe.

student • girl • language • car • city • boy

1 I have one ...., Gary, and two ...., Diane and Sally.
2 We have two ...., a BMW and a Mini.
3 I am in a class with eight ....
4 English, French and Italian are European ....
5 Bristol and Manchester are .... in England.

5 **Make sentences using the information in the chart.**
Bilden Sie Sätze aus den Informationen in der Tabelle.

	question	answer
1	speak English?	✓
2	drive?	✗
3	ski?	✓
4	cook spaghetti?	✓
5	swim?	✗
6	play cricket?	✗

1 Can you .... ? Yes, I can.
2 .... ? No, I can't.
3 .... ? Yes, ...
4 .... ? ....
5 .... ? No, ...
6 .... ? ....

6 **Look at the pie charts with information about Greg and Mandy. Then decide who says each sentence.**
Sehen Sie sich die Diagramme mit den Informationen zu Greg und Mandy an. Entscheiden Sie dann, wer welchen Satz sagt.

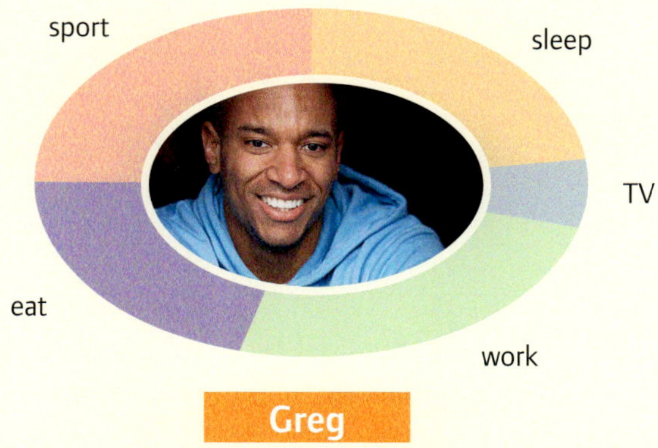

		Mandy	Greg
1	"I sleep a lot."		
2	"When I'm home in the evening, I watch a little TV."		
3	"I work a lot. I'm the boss!"		
4	"On Friday I work for a couple of hours in a restaurant."		
5	"I don't eat a lot."		
6	"I don't have time to read."		
7	"I like sport and I play in a football team on Saturdays and Sundays. It's great."		
8	"I watch TV for about 30 minutes in the evening. That's all."		
9	"I watch TV a lot. I love it."		
10	"I don't play sport."		

7 1.17 **Listen to this interview and complete the form.**
Hören Sie das Interview an und füllen Sie das Formular aus.

1 Do you know Italy?
____

2 When do you go to Italy?
____

3 Where do you go in Italy?
____

4 Can you speak Italian?
____

5 Do you like Italian food?
____

6 Do you have Italian friends?
____

Key classroom language

- Are you sure?
- Can you help me, please?
- I'm not sure.
- Can I work with you?
- No problem.
- Is that right?
- Great, thanks a lot.
- Sorry, I don't understand.
- Right.

4 A That's delicious!

Delicious!

1 Match the words to the pictures.
Ordnen Sie die Begriffe den Bildern zu.

spaghetti • burger and chips • curry and rice • omelette • pizza • fruit salad • paella • chicken salad

Add these comments to the pictures.
Fügen Sie diese Kommentare den Bildern hinzu.

- Lovely!
- Delicious!
- I like that.
- My favourite.
- I don't like that.
- It's horrible.
- Not for me, thanks.

Ready to order?

2 Complete the dialogues with the name of the dishes.
Ergänzen Sie die Dialoge mit den passenden Gerichten.

1
Nick: What's in the ....?
Waiter: Oh, chicken, vegetables and sauce.
Nick: Is it hot?
Waiter: Yes, it is.

2
Kim: That looks nice. What's in it?
Shop assistant: In the ....? It's rice with meat and fish and vegetables. It's Spanish.

3
Andy: What's in the ....?
Waitress: Onions and mushrooms.
Andy: No meat?
Waitress: No. Just vegetables.
Andy: Lovely. I'm a vegetarian.

4
Vicky: What's in the ....?
Jim: Apples, oranges, bananas and kiwi fruit.
Vicky: Delicious. My favourites.

5
Waiter: Here you are.
Luke: Lovely ...., my favourite.
Waiter: Right. Do you want ketchup or mayonnaise? Salt?
Luke: Salt and pepper, please.

Write a dialogue for another dish and read it out. Which dish is it?
Schreiben Sie einen Dialog zu einem anderen Gericht und lesen Sie ihn vor. Welches Gericht ist es?

→ 49

Do you like cheese? Yes, I **do**.
But Sam **doesn't**. He **doesn't** eat cheese.
Luke **doesn't** eat meat. He is a vegetarian.
Does paella have meat in it? Yes, it **does**.
What **does** 'Senf' mean? It means 'mustard'.

3 Answer the questions.

Beantworten Sie die Fragen.

Yes he/she does
No, he/she doesn't.
Yes, it does.

1 Does the omelette have meat?
2 Does Andy eat meat?
3 Does Andy eat an omelette?
4 Does spaghetti come from Spain?

5 1.18 Listen to these conversations and answer the questions.

Hören Sie die Gespräche an und beantworten Sie die Fragen.

1

Tina drinks … ☐ mineral water ☐ wine ☐ beer
Phil drinks … ☐ mineral water ☐ wine ☐ beer

2

1 Who doesn't eat fish?
☐ Lucy doesn't ☐ Pete doesn't
2 Who wants paella?
☐ Lucy does ☐ Pete does
3 What do they drink?
☐ beer ☐ coke ☐ wine ☐ mineral water

6 And finally … Put the words in the right order, then ask and answer the questions.

Bringen Sie die Satzteile in die korrekte Reihenfolge und beantworten Sie die Fragen.

Food interview

1 Do … you | fish | like ?
2 Can … cook | you ?
3 Are … vegetarian | you | a ?
4 Where … restaurant | your | favourite | is ?
5 What … your | favourite | drink | is ?
6 Do … the | in | morning | eat | you ?
7 What … don't | food | like | you ?
8 What … food | is | favourite | your ?

Food & drink

4 Complete the mind map.

Ergänzen Sie die Übersicht.

oranges • carrots • chips • fruit juice • potatoes • wine • kebabs • strawberries • chicken

Tell your partner about your favourite thing in each category.

Nennen Sie Ihrem Partner Ihr Lieblingsessen oder -getränk aus jeder Kategorie.

My favourite … is …

food & drink

- fruit: apples, bananas, grapes, ___, ___
- fast food: hamburgers, pizzas, hot dogs, ___, ___

- vegetables: onions, tomatoes, beans, ___, ___
- drinks: tea, coffee, milk, beer, mineral water, ___, ___

- meat: beef, lamb, pork, ___

4 B Shopping

1 Match the pictures and the words.

Ordnen Sie die Begriffe den passenden Bildern zu.

1 shoes
2 post office
3 clothes
4 supermarket
5 travel agent
6 books
7 online shopping

2 1.19 Listen to these conversations and write the name of the person (M, V or S) in the correct place.

Hören Sie die Dialoge an und notieren Sie den Namen (M, V oder S) an der richtigen Stelle.

shopping	I love it	It's OK	No, I hate it
for food	☐	☐	☐
for clothes	☐	☐	☐
for shoes	☐	☐	☐
for books or music	☐	☐	☐
for holidays	☐	☐	☐

Matt

Vic

Sally

3 1.19 Listen again and make questions.

Hören Sie die Dialoge noch einmal an und bilden Sie Fragen.

1 do | you | like | shopping?
2 what | favourite | shop?
3 do | like | supermarkets?
4 do | like | shopping | online?
5 where | buy | books?

Ask and answer the questions.

Stellen Sie die Fragen und beantworten Sie diese.

Where can I buy …?

4 Match the two parts.

Ordnen Sie die Begriffe zu.

I want to buy …	You can go to the …
stamps	butcher
aspirin	newsagent
sausages	post office
bread	shoe shop
newspapers	chemist
shoes	baker

True (✔) or false (✘)?

Richtig oder falsch?

1 You can get stamps from a butcher.
2 You can get chicken from a newsagent.
3 You can get aspirin from a chemist.
4 You can get newspapers from the baker.
5 You can get almost everything from a supermarket.

Correct the sentences that are false.

Korrigieren Sie die Sätze, die falsch sind.

5 **Look at the map of the shopping centre and match the questions and answers.**
Sehen Sie sich die Übersicht des Einkaufszentrums an. Ordnen Sie die Fragen den korrekten Antworten zu.

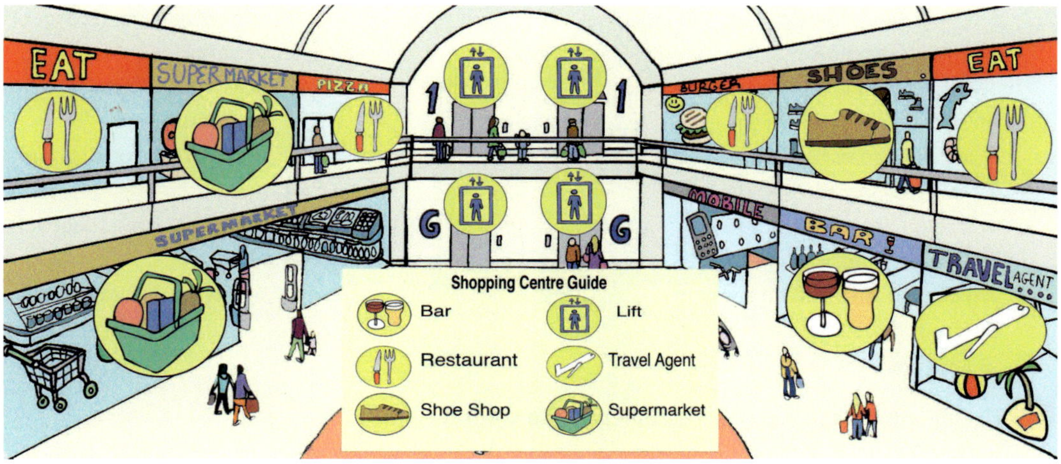

1 Is there a car park here?
2 Is there a bar here?
3 Is there a restaurant here?
4 Is there a supermarket here?
5 Is there a lift?
6 Is there a travel agent here?
7 Is there a shoe shop?

A Yes, there are lots upstairs.
B Yes, there is.
C No, there isn't.
D Yes, there is. It's upstairs.
E Yes, there are four.
F Yes, there is.
G Yes, there are two.

→ 49

Is there a bank near here? No, **there isn't**.
There are lots of restaurants in this street.
Excuse me. **Is there** a post office here? Yes, **there's** a post office in Market Street.

6 **You are a tourist. What questions do you ask in these situations?**
Welche Fragen stellen Sie als Tourist(in) in diesen Situationen?

1 You want to buy stamps for a postcard.
2 You want to change money.
3 You want to eat.
4 You want to buy shoes.
5 You want to see a film.

Ask and answer the questions about the area where you live.
Stellen Sie die Fragen und beantworten Sie diese über die Gegend, in der Sie wohnen.

7 **Fill the gaps with these missing words.**
Füllen Sie die Lücken mit den passenden Wörtern.

cost • know • help • pay • much • looking • there

1 – Can I ………… you?
– I'm just …………, thanks.

2 – How much does that ………….
– £25.10.

3 – Can I ………… by credit card?
– Of course, no problem.

4 – Thank you very …………
– You're welcome.

5 – Is … a bank near here?
– Sorry, I don't …………. I'm a tourist.

8 **And finally …** **Make these sentences true for you.**
Ändern Sie die Sätze so, dass diese auf Sie zutreffen.

1 There are no good restaurants where I live.
2 There's a post office near here.
3 You can buy stamps, shoes, beer, food and clothes from a supermarket.
4 I love shopping.
5 There are four supermarkets near here.
6 There's a nice park near where I live.

4 C Homestudy

1 Match the food to the description.

Verbinden Sie die Beschreibungen mit dem passenden Gericht.

1 This is hot. They eat it a lot in India.
2 This is from Italy. I like it with lots of cheese.
3 This is lots of nice things – apples, bananas, grapes.
4 They eat this a lot in Spain. There's rice and meat in it.
5 This is my favourite. I eat this with tomato ketchup.
6 This is difficult to eat! It's Italian.

- fruit salad
- pizza
- burger and chips
- spaghetti
- curry and rice
- paella

4 Which things are in the wrong place?

Was passt nicht in die Reihe?

1 **fruit**
apples | bananas | oranges | fruit juice | strawberries

2 **vegetables**
peas | grapes | onions | tomatoes | beans | carrots | potatoes

3 **fast food**
lamb | hamburgers | pizzas | hot dogs | kebabs

4 **drinks**
tea | coffee | milk | beer | mineral water | lettuce | wine

5 **meat**
beef | chips | chicken | pork

2 Decide who is talking, the customer or the waiter?

Entscheiden Sie, wer hier spricht – der Gast oder der Kellner?

		customer	waiter
1	Can I help you?	☐	☐
2	I'm a vegetarian.	☐	☐
3	What would you like?	☐	☐
4	This is delicious, thank you.	☐	☐
5	What's in it?	☐	☐
6	Here you are.	☐	☐
7	Are you ready to order?	☐	☐
8	Mineral water, please.	☐	☐
9	Chicken salad for me, I think.	☐	☐
10	Here's the menu.	☐	☐

3 Match the questions and answers.

Ordnen Sie die Fragen den passenden Antworten zu.

1 Do vegetarians eat chicken?
2 Do they eat a lot of rice in China?
3 Does wine come from France?
4 Are hamburgers a type of fast food?
5 Do you have milk in your coffee?
6 Can you get fish and chips in London?
7 Are tomatoes a type of meat?
8 Does paella come from Germany?

A Yes, it does.
B Yes, you can.
C No, it doesn't.
D No, they don't.
E Yes, they are.
F No, they aren't.
G Yes, I do.
H Yes, they do.

5 1.20 **Look at the menu. Listen and write down what the people order.**

Sehen Sie sich die Speisekarte an. Hören Sie dann den Dialog und notieren Sie, was die Gäste bestellen.

Len: ……………………………………………………………….

Alice: ……………………………………………………………….

6 **True (✓) or false (✗)?**

Richtig oder falsch?

1 You can get meat from a ~~travel agent~~. ✗
butcher
2 You can get bread from the baker.
……………………………………………………………….
3 You can get sausages from a supermarket.
……………………………………………………………….
4 You can get newspapers from a chemist.
……………………………………………………………….
5 You can't get holidays from a shoe shop.
……………………………………………………………….
6 You can get aspirin from a butcher.
……………………………………………………………….

Correct the sentences that are false.

Korrigieren Sie die Fehler.

7 **Match the two parts.**

Verbinden Sie die Sätze.

1 Can I help you?
2 How much does that cost?
3 Can I pay by credit card?
4 Thank you very much.
5 Is there a bank near here?
6 Can I buy food, drink and clothes near here?

A Sorry, I can't help you. I'm a tourist.
B You're welcome.
C Yes, there's a supermarket in that street.
D Sorry, I don't know. I don't work here.
E Of course, no problem.
F I'm just looking, thanks.

Key classroom language

- Sorry, I don't know.
- Can I ask a question?
- What's the answer to number four?
- There's a small problem.
- What about you?
- Have a good weekend.
- What does that mean?
- That's easy.
- That's my favourite.
- Do you agree?

New York City, USA
Donuts
I just like the colours!

Parma, Italy
Pigs' legs
Pigs' legs hang for month or years and become 'prosciutto'.

Chicago, USA
Sushi rolls
Japanese food is very popular in Chicago and it gets here fast and fresh!

Stockholm, Sweden
Semla
The traditional food on "Fat Tuesday" in autumn.

Costa Rica
Fried whole fish
Our own fish fried for us!

Buenos Aires, Argentina
Gyro (roast lamb) spit
From an "International Festival". The world's people are blending!

Jerusalem, Israel
Pistachio Pastries
From the Mehane Yehuda Market.

Eilat, Israel
Bagel with smoked salmon
A taste of home for me!

"I love food! And now, the more I travel, the more it becomes about the food. From local markets to gourmet grocery shops to tasty street food – I love it all!"

Lisa Lubin, world traveller, TV producer and photographer

Cancale, France
Fresh Oysters
Fresh out of the water!

Berlin, Germany
Currywurst
To me, a hot dog with ketchup and curry powder!

Dalat, Vietnam
Chicken Feet
Every part of the animal is used here.

Dubai, U.A.E
McDonald's in a shopping mall
I just like the sign in Arabic.

Melbourne, Australia
Caramels
Little girl dreaming of sweets!

popular – beliebt, populär; **(to) get here** – hierher gelangen; **fat** – dick, fett; **legs** – Beine; **(to) hang** – hängen; **autumn** – Herbst; **is used** – wird verwendet; **(to) blend** – vermischen

My favourite foods

I love learning about cultures and countries via food. You can learn a lot about a country by eating and drinking with the local people. People talk, share food and become friends over a drink, a bag of crisps or in a cafe. Here are some of my favourite dishes from around the world! Bon appétit!

1 In the USA, I love cheeseburgers and French fries and beer from my favourite bar 'The Scoreboard' in Quincy, Illinois, USA.
2 In Italy, my favourite food is 'Bigolli con Arne', which is fat pasta noodles with a duck sauce and my favourite drink is 'Spritz con Aperol' - white wine, bubble water and orange liquor. You can find it in Vicenza, Italy.
3 When I am in Brazil, I like to eat 'feijoada' or Bean Stew with rice and fried bananas. I like a fresh exotic fruit juice made of star fruit.
4 In Lisbon, Portugal, I like custard tarts called 'Pastel de Belem' that you find only in the Belem district of the city. They are very tasty with powdered sugar and cinnamon.
5 My favourite sweet in Spain is 'churros'. They are little Spanish donuts that you dip in a thick hot chocolate drink. They are good for sharing.

learning a lot – viel über etwas lernen; **eating and drinking** – essen und trinken; **(to) share** – teilen; **French fries** – Pommes; **fat pasta noodles** – dicke Pastanudeln; **duck sauce** – Entensoße; **bubble water** – sprudelndes Wasser; **Bean Stew** – Bohneneintopf; **rice** – Reis; **fried bananas** – frittierte Bananen; **star fruit** – Sternfrucht; **custard tart** – Eiercremetörtchen; **district** – Bezirk; **tasty** – geschmackvoll, aromatisch; **powdered sugar** – Puderzucker; **cinnamon** – Zimt; **sweet** – Süßigkeit; **thick** – dick, zähflüssig

5 A At home

At home

1 What room is it? Tick (✔) the correct box.
Welches Zimmer ist es? Kreuzen Sie die richtige Box an.

☐ bedroom ☐ bathroom

☐ kitchen ☐ bedroom

☐ bathroom
☐ hall

☐ living room
☐ hall

☐ garden ☐ winter garden

☐ hall ☐ living room

2 Match the descriptions to the families.
Ordnen Sie die Beschreibungen den Familien zu.

"We live in a small flat."

"We live in a big house."

1 This is my home. I love it. It's modern. There are two bedrooms, one for me and my wife, and one for David, our son.

2 The kitchen is modern, but we don't eat in it. It has a washing machine, fridge, cooker, but there isn't a table.

3 We eat in the living room. The sofa is a sofa-bed so the living room can be a bedroom when friends come.

4 There's a large bathroom with a bath and a shower.

5 We've got a TV and computer in the living room, and a TV in the bedroom.

6 I love the kitchen. It's a lovely, big room with a big kitchen table. We eat in the kitchen.

7 The computer and TV are in the living room. It's my favourite room. We've got a nice garden.

8 I love the balcony, because we haven't got a garden.

→ 50

I**'ve got** a computer in my bedroom.
I **haven't got** a TV. I don't like TV.
Have you **got** a garden? Yes, I have.
The house **has got** two bedrooms.

3 What's in your home? Complete this table.

Was haben Sie zu Hause? Füllen Sie die Tabelle aus.

	TV	shower	sofa	table	computer	washing machine	fridge
bedroom	☐	☐	☐	☐	☐	☐	☐
living room	☐	☐	☐	☐	☐	☐	☐
kitchen	☐	☐	☐	☐	☐	☐	☐
garden	☐	☐	☐	☐	☐	☐	☐
balcony	☐	☐	☐	☐	☐	☐	☐
hall	☐	☐	☐	☐	☐	☐	☐
bathroom	☐	☐	☐	☐	☐	☐	☐

Are these sentences true (✔) or false (✘) for you?

Treffen diese Sätze auf Sie zu oder nicht?

1. I've got a TV in the bedroom.
2. My home has got three bedrooms.
3. I've got a sofa in the hall.
4. I haven't got a washing machine.
5. The bedrooms are upstairs.
6. I eat in the living room.

Change the sentences that are wrong.

Ändern Sie die Sätze so, dass diese auf Sie zutreffen.

4 Complete these questions.

Ergänzen Sie die Fragen.

1. Have you got a .... in your home?
2. Do you live in a .... or a flat?
3. How many .... are there in your home?
4. Where is the .... in your home?
5. Where .... eat?
6. What's in the .... in your home?

→ 51

How many books have you got at home?
How many people are in the English class?

Ask your partner about his/her home.

Stellen Sie Ihrem Partner Fragen über sein/ihr Zuhause.

5 1.21 Who talks about these rooms?

Wer spricht über diese Räume?

Jane talks about a …
Max doesn't talk about …

bathroom · bedroom · garden · gym · kitchen · hall · toilet · swimming pool · living room

Jane

Nick

Max

Complete these sentences.

Vervollständigen Sie diese Sätze.

1. **Jane:** My favourite room is my ....
2. **Nick:** My favourite place at home is ....
3. **Max:** I don't live in a .... I live in a ....

6 And finally … What's your favourite room?

Was ist Ihr Lieblingszimmer?

- Tell your partner about your favourite room at home.
- Tell him/her about three things you've got at home.

My favourite room is my …
I like it because it is … / there are …/
I've got a …
There's a … in my home.

5 B Me, my family and my things

Who is who?

1 **Write the names of the people in the pictures.**
Notieren Sie die Namen der Personen auf den Bildern.

This is me, Claire, and my family. You can see me and Jim, my husband. He's 43. We've got two children, Tammy and Simon. Tammy is 15. We are mother and daughter, but we are also friends. We listen to the same music, we've got the same hairstyle, and we like the same clothes. People say to me, 'Claire, is Tammy your sister?' Simon, our son, is 11. He loves football, and he loves Russ. Who's Russ? He's our dog. He's one of the family, too.

I'm Gary, and Sally is my wife. June is her mother. She lives with us now. She's 62, and she cooks great food! We've got three children. You can see Billy here. He's 3. His two brothers, Mark and Olly, are not in the photo. They are 18 and 19, and they are at university, so they don't live here now.

2 **True (✔) or false (✘)?**
Richtig oder falsch?

1 Jim and Claire have got two children.
2 Simon has got one brother.
3 Sally and her family have got a dog.
4 Sally is June's mother.
5 Mark and Olly are brother and sister.
6 Billy has got one brother and one sister.
7 Claire and Tammy are sisters.
8 Sally and Gary and Claire and Jim have got one daughter.

→ 51

June is Sally**'s** mother.
Tammy is Claire**'s** daughter.
My sister**'s** name is Anne.

3 **Who is …**
Wer ist …

1 June's daughter?
2 Tammy's brother?
3 Jim's wife?
4 Simon's father?
5 Simon's sister?
6 Sally's husband?

Make two more questions and test your partner.
Bilden Sie zwei weitere Fragen und stellen Sie diese Ihrem Partner.

4 **Make these sentences true for you.**
Ändern Sie die Sätze so, dass diese auf Sie zutreffen.

1 I've got two brothers.
2 My father's name is Jon, and my mother's name is Wendy.
3 I've got no children.
4 I don't like animals, so we haven't got a dog or a cat at home.
5 I'm a grandparent.
6 I live with my parents.

Tell your partner about your family.
Berichten Sie Ihrem Partner über Ihre Familie.

5 1.22 **Listen to the dialogues and decide which picture the people are talking about.**
Hören Sie die Dialoge an und entscheiden Sie, über welches Bild die Personen gerade sprechen.

6 Choose the correct word.

Wählen Sie das passende Wort aus.

1 This is a photo of me and my | her mum. His | Her name is Pam.
2 This is a photo of my brother and her | his wife with their | our three children.
3 Does your | my sister live with her | your parents?
4 This is Phil and me in our | her new car.
5 What's our | your favourite day of the week?

→ 51

This is **my** bag.	*I – my*
What's in **your** bag?	*you – your*
This is John's briefcase and **his** things are in it.	*he – his*
Nina has a photo of **her** brother.	*she – her*
This is a photo of **our** English class.	*we – our*
This is a photo of **my** parents in **their** garden.	*they – their*

7 Match the words to the pictures.

Ordnen Sie die Begriffe den Gegenständen zu.

1 mirror 2 mobile 3 keys 4 perfume 5 hairbrush 6 pen 7 glasses 8 laptop 9 bus ticket 10 purse / wallet 11 lipstick 12 umbrella

In my bag …

8 Are these sentences true for you?

Treffen diese Sätze auf Sie zu?

1 I haven't got a photo of my family with me.
2 I haven't got a purse in my bag.
3 I've got my umbrella in my briefcase.
4 I've got my glasses in my pocket.
5 I've got some money in my pocket.

→ 50

a restaurant, **a** newspaper = *ein/e/r*
some shoes, **some** newspapers = *einige*

9 Put one object each on the teacher's desk. Can you remember all the objects and who they belong to?

Legen Sie alle je einen Gegenstand auf einen Tisch. Können Sie sich an alle Gegenstände und Besitzer erinnern?

That's Maria's laptop. *I think that's Gunther's book.*

10 And finally … How many true sentences can you make in two minutes?

Wie viele passende Sätze über sich können Sie in zwei Minuten bilden?

I	have haven't	got	a some my	keys perfume laptop bus ticket book glasses purse/wallet lipstick mobile	in my	pocket. bag. briefcase. rucksack.

Make three questions.

Bilden Sie drei Fragen.

Have you got a/some/your … with you?

Ask and answer the questions with your partner.

Stellen Sie die Fragen und beantworten Sie diese.

5 C Homestudy

1 Unscramble the coloured words.
Entknoten Sie die farbig markierten Wörter.

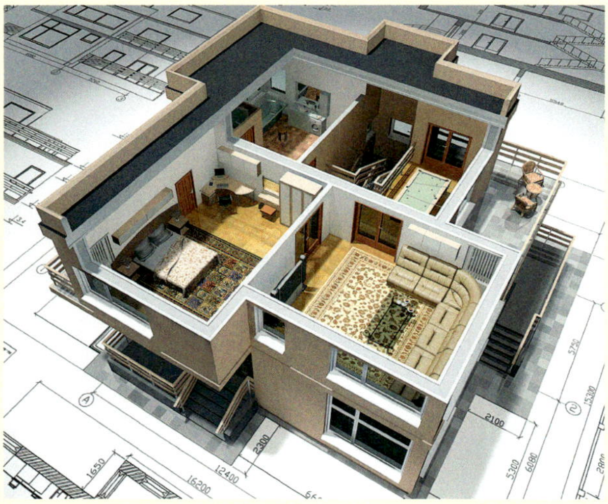

1 There's a o l t i e t in the bathroom.

……………………………………………

2 The kitchen is where you find the e r o c o k .

……………………………………………

3 We have a bathroom with a s w e r h o .

……………………………………………

4 My clothes are in the s h i n w a g machine.

……………………………………………

5 The milk is in the r i g f e d . ……………………

6 I don't have a f s a o in my bedroom, but there's one in the living room. ……………………

2 Add the missing words to these questions.
Ergänzen Sie die Fragen mit den fehlenden Wörtern.

Do • Have • Have • Do • Where • How

1 …………………… you got a shower in your home?
2 …………………… you live in a house or a flat?
3 …………………… many bedrooms are there in your home?
4 …………………… are the bedrooms in your home?
5 …………………… you eat in the kitchen?
6 …………………… you got a balcony?

3 Decide which form completes the sentences.
Mit welchem Wort können Sie die Sätze ergänzen?

1 I don't like animal's | animals.
2 What's | Whats your father's | fathers name?
3 I have got two sisters | sister's.
4 Where's | Wheres Jacks | Jack's car?
5 On Saturday I play football with my friends | friend's for two or three hour's | hours.

4 Match the words to the pictures.
Ordnen Sie die Begriffe den Bildern zu.

1 glasses
2 keys
3 money
4 laptop
5 passport
6 umbrella
7 tickets
8 tissues

A

B

C

D
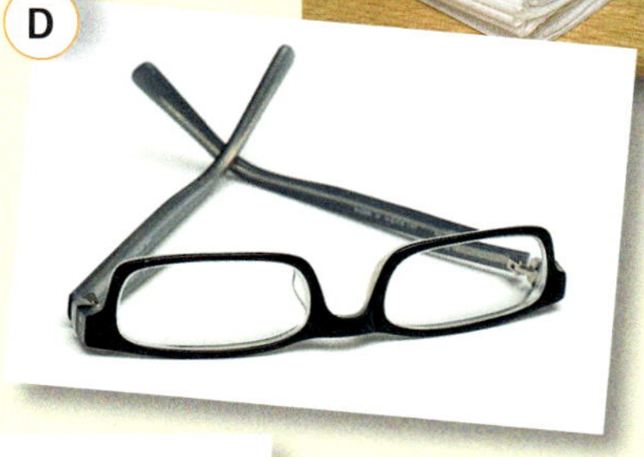

E

F

G

H

5 1.23 Listen. Tick (✔) the things Don and June have got.
Hören Sie sich den Dialog an. Setzen Sie einen Haken bei den Gegenständen, die Don und June haben.

6 Match the greetings and the pictures.

Ordnen Sie die Grüße dem entsprechenden Bild zu.

A

B

C

D

E

1 Congratulations on your new family!

2 Please come to our party!

3 I hope the year is a good one for you and your family!

4 Good luck with your exams!

5 Have a wonderful time on your special day!

7 Who is who?

Wer ist wer?

Who is/are …

1 your father's wife?

2 your parents' parents?

3 your children's children?

4 your children's grandparents?

5 your parents' children?

6 your parents' daughter?

- ☐ Your sister
- ☐ You, your brothers and sisters
- ☐ Your grandchildren
- ☐ Your mother
- ☐ Your parents
- ☐ Your grandparents

8 Make logical sentences.

Bilden Sie logische Sätze.

1 This is a photo of me and …
2 Sorry. I can't remember …
3 This is Pablo and …
4 I know Maria, but I don't know …
5 Georgina is a doctor, and …
6 This is Nancy and me, with Tom and Jill, …
7 I love Tom Hanks. I think this is …

A her husband.
B his best film.
C our children.
D her father is one, too.
E my mum. Her name is Phoebe.
F his wife, Patricia.
G your name.

Key classroom language

- OK, let's start.
- It's really nice.
- I don't think so.
- Time to go home.
- Have you got a question?
- That's interesting.
- It's pretty good.

6 A Public and private transport

1 Look at the pictures and the words. Which words are in the wrong boxes?

Sehen Sie sich die Bilder und die Begriffe an. Welche Wörter sind in der falschen Box?

bus	plane	ship
bike	foot	car
under-ground	train	tram

Put the means of transport into categories:

Ordnen Sie die Verkehrsmittel diesen Kategorien zu:

2 Complete these sentences.

Vervollständigen Sie die Sätze.

1 Buses are cheap but slow. .... are fast but expensive.
2 In Paris the .... is the 'metro'.
3 Trains are fast, but .... aren't.
4 Buses aren't private transport, but .... are.
5 Bikes are a green type of transport, but .... aren't.
6 You can go from the UK to France by plane, train and ....
7 In big cities I take buses, trams or the underground. In small cities I walk. I go on ....

3 Answer the questions with a partner.

Beantworten Sie die Fragen mit einem Partner.

1 Can you go from Germany to France by bus?
2 Can you travel from the UK to Ireland by train?
3 What do they use for the 'Tour de France'?
4 Can you go from Europe to North America by plane in three hours?
5 Do you need a passport to go from England to Scotland by train?
6 Can you get home from your English class by public transport in 20 minutes?

→ 51

We **always** go to France on holiday.
We **never** fly – we **normally** drive, but **sometimes** we take the train.

4 Decide if the statements are true (✔) or false (✘).

Entscheiden Sie, ob die Aussagen richtig oder falsch sind.

1 I always speak English in class.
2 I never take the train.
3 I sometimes drive to work.
4 I normally go home on foot after my English class.
5 I don't drink and drive. I normally take a taxi.
6 Sometimes I take the underground to work, and sometimes I take the tram.

Tell your partner your real answers.

Geben Sie Ihrem Partner Ihre richtigen Antworten.

Chicago Train Red Line

5 Match the sentences with the same meaning.

Verbinden Sie die Sätze mit der gleichen Bedeutung.

1 I sometimes drive to work.
2 I sometimes fly.
3 I always walk everywhere.
4 I take the bus most days.
5 There are boats every day.
6 I normally go by bike.

A I sometimes go by plane.
B You can always sail.
C I cycle a lot, but not every day.
D I sometimes go to work by car.
E I never drive. I go on foot.
F I normally go by bus.

6 1.24 Listen and write down the types of transport you hear.

Hören Sie zu und notieren Sie die Verkehrsmittel in der Reihenfolge, in der diese genannt werden.

taxi • car • underground • train • ~~plane~~ • boat

1 *plane* ....
2 ....
3 ....
4 ....
5 ....
6 ....

1.24 Listen again and put them in the order Kelly uses them.

Hören Sie den Dialog noch einmal an und ordnen Sie die Verkehrsmittel nun in der Reihenfolge, in der Kelly diese benutzt.

1 ....
2 ....
3 ....
4 ....
5 ....
6 ....

7 Look at the map of the Chicago underground and answer the questions.

Sehen Sie sich den U-Bahnplan aus Chicago an und beantworten Sie die Fragen.

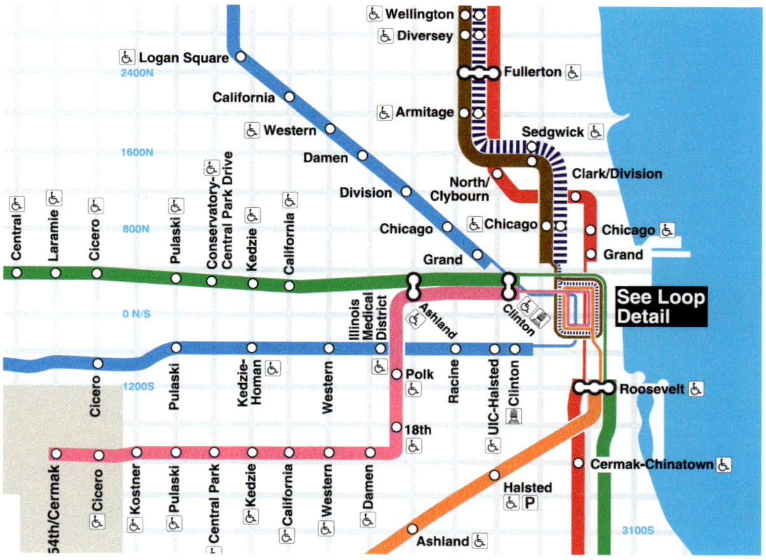

1 Excuse me, which line goes to 'Halsted'?
2 Can I take the blue line to 'Racine'?
3 Does the green line go to the 'Illinois Medical District'?
4 Do the red and brown lines go to 'Roosevelt', where my hotel is?
5 My sister lives near 'Clinton'. Which lines go there?
6 Is 'Logan Square' on the pink line?

8 Match the two parts

Verbinden Sie die Fragen und Antworten.

1 Can I get to the hotel by bus?
2 How much is a ticket?
3 When does the train leave?
4 Do you travel first class?
5 Have you got the car here?
6 Do you go to work by car?
7 Which bus goes to the station?
8 Is there a car park near here?

A The number 86, I think.
B No, you can't, but you can take a taxi.
C No, never. I always take the bus.
D No, we don't. It's expensive.
E Sorry, I don't know.
F About £5.
G At 6.30.
H Yes, I have.

9 And finally ... Ask and answer the questions with your partner.

Stellen Sie Ihrem Partner Fragen und beantworten Sie diese.

In your family, who ...

- hasn't got a car?
- walks to the shops?
- doesn't drive to work?
- never goes by plane?
- sometimes cycles?
- normally travels by public transport?

6 B My holidays

1 Add the missing months and seasons.

Ergänzen Sie die fehlenden Jahreszeiten und Monate.

autumn • June • May • winter • November • August

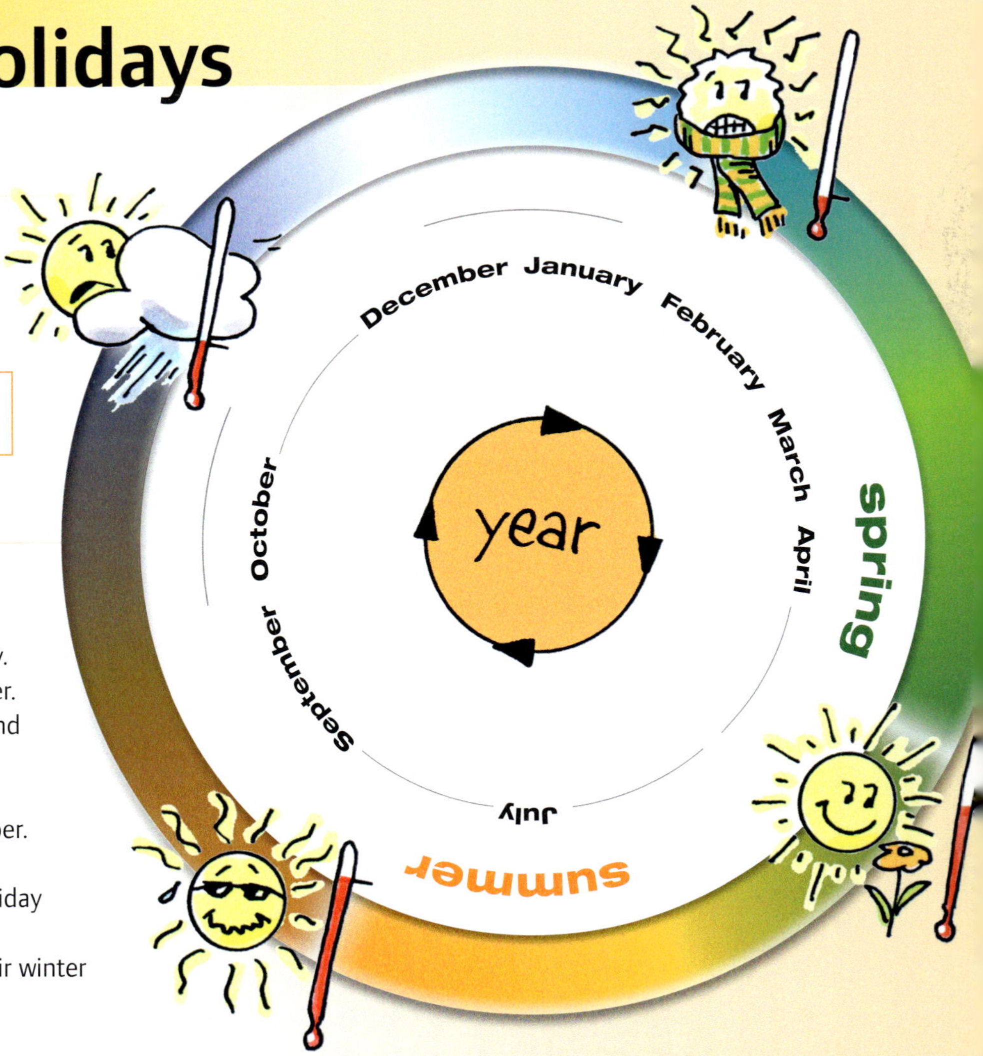

2 Correct these sentences.

Korrigieren Sie die Sätze.

1 The New Year starts in February.
2 Christmas is always in November.
3 Easter is sometimes in March and sometimes in April.
4 My favourite season is winter.
5 My favourite month is September.
6 My birthday is in June.
7 I normally have my summer holiday in December.
8 A lot of people go skiing in their winter holidays.

3 Match the descriptions to the places and seasons.

Ordnen Sie die Beschreibungen den Orten bzw. Jahreszeiten zu.

1 The trees are red, gold, green and yellow.
2 It rains a lot and it's cold.
3 It's very hot and sunny.
4 It snows a lot and it's cold.
5 It's not hot and not cold, and everything is green.

A Switzerland in spring.
B Egypt in summer.
C Sweden in winter.
D New England in the autumn.
E England in the winter.

Talking about the weather

4 Match the two parts.

Verbinden Sie die Satzhälften.

1 Does it
2 What can you do
3 Does it always snow here
4 Is the weather
5 Is it

A good today?
B normally sunny here in November?
C rain here a lot?
D in winter?
E here in the summer?

Ask and answer the questions.

Stellen Sie einander die Fragen und beantworten Sie diese.

5 Match the different things you need to the different types of holiday.

Ordnen Sie die Dinge den Urlaubsarten zu.

map | guide book | sunglasses | bag | money | towel | gloves | scarf | hat | skis | bikini | food | tent | torch | warm clothes | sleeping bag

What is the right holiday for these people?

Welcher Urlaub passt zu wem?

1 I like culture – museums and films and things. Places like Paris and New York are fantastic.
2 I want to relax in the sun, read a book, do nothing for hours, and swim in the sea when I feel hot.
3 My favourite country is Austria, because I love the snow, and I love sport.
4 I don't like hotels and busy cities with lots of shops and noise and people. I like the country, and simple things. And I haven't got a lot of money.
5 For me, it's theatre, restaurants, theatre, restaurants. That's a perfect holiday.

6 1.25 Listen. Who likes which holiday?

Hören Sie zu – wer bevorzugt welche Art von Urlaub?

1 Alison 

2 Ian and Ian's wife 

3 Marie 

7 Complete these sentences about you.

Ergänzen Sie die Sätze über sich.

1 My favourite type of holidays are … holidays.
2 My favourite countries for holidays are … and … .
3 When I'm on holiday, I never … .
4 I always take my … and … when I go on holiday.
5 I never take … or … when I go on holiday.
6 I normally go on holiday in … .

8 And finally … Look at the words below and put them in a logical order for you (*like* ⇨ *don't like*).

Sehen Sie sich die Begriffe unten an und bringen Sie diese in eine für Sie logische Reihenfolge.

summer | a holiday with family | cheap holidays | sport | city breaks | Spain | a holiday with friends | beer | culture | **or** | planes | spring | books | autumn | expensive holidays | boats | films | France | beach holidays | winter | wine

Interview your partner and ask questions. What's the perfect holiday destination for you?

Stellen Sie Ihrem Partner Fragen. Was ist das perfekte Urlaubsziel für Sie?

Do you like summer or winter?
Do you like boats or planes?

6 C Homestudy

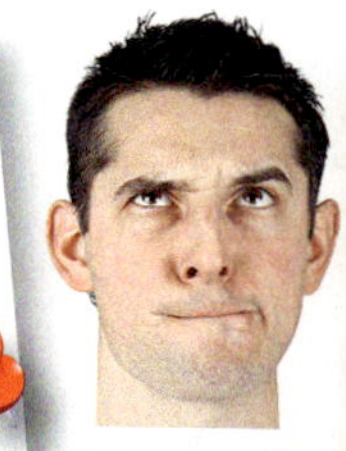

I can … ☺ 😐 ☹

Unit 1
- greet someone
- say who I am and where I'm from

Unit 2
- spell my name
- give my telephone number
- ask and answer questions about parts of a city

Unit 3
- talk about what I like and don't like
- name some activities
- talk about food I like

Unit 4
- talk about shops and shopping
- say where I can buy certain things

Unit 5
- talk about rooms at home
- tell someone what I've got at home

Unit 6
- talk about public transport and travel
- make holiday plans

ABC
THIS IS MY
Goodge Street
Holborn
Tottenham Court Road
Leicester Square
Charing Cross
Afgange Departures
Time New Time Destination Flight Gate Remarks
1450 Amsterdam AF8428 11 Final call
1455 Dublin FR873 4 Final call
1500 Varna BUC3558 13 Go to gate
1535 Copenhagen SK8344 8
1545 Monastir SK7715 15
1605 Munich LH9975 5
1620 Rome CIA NB835 10
1650 Manchester BA8247 14
1650 Oslo AY5887 7
Time New Time Destination Flight Gate
1700 Bourgas NB991 13
1700 Stockholm SK3447 11
1710 London LGW NB813 15
1740 Amsterdam KL1348 12
1810 Copenhagen SK8346 8
1820 Stavanger DX025 11
1825 Frankfurt LH9477 10
2045 Copenhagen SK8348
2100 Antalya
coffee
bananas
milk
spaghetti
salad

Planes
There are over 21 million aircraft departures every day worldwide. Approximately 500,000 people are "in the air" while you read this. Only 6 astronauts are in space. On average, we all fly 317 kilometres a year.

Trains
Each year, people travel 2.2 trillion kilometres by train. Each person travels 358 kilometres a year by train.

Cars
There are 590 million cars in the world. There are 140 million cars in the U.S., 55 million in Japan, 9 million in China and 6 million in India.

public transport

"The lines show the ambiguity of modern travelling and transport: the pleasure, but also the restlessness."

Frank Maier, illustrator

TOP 5 TOURIST DESTINATIONS (countries)

France • United States • Spain • China • Italy

TOP 5 TOURIST DESTINATIONS (cities)

New York • Los Angeles • Las Vegas • London • San Francisco

Other popular cities in the **TOP 50**

Paris (13), Barcelona (14), Madrid (17), Rome (21), Istanbul (30), Palma de Mallorca (35), Amsterdam (36), Athens (38), Zurich (40) and Berlin (42).

Transport tips for travellers

The train (or bus) station can be confusing in a new country. Where is my train? Do I have the right ticket? Which stop is mine? There are many possible problems. Here are a few tips for the train (or bus) for your next trip!

1 When you buy a train or a bus ticket, write down the destination, the time of the train (or bus), and the date you travel. You can go to the bus or train station and show them the piece of paper.
2 On an overnight train or bus, bring a pair of earplugs so you can sleep.
3 A good map! But don't be afraid to ask directions. Many people get lost and sometimes it is best to ask a local where you are or where to go. They can show you on the map.
4 Check the stations before and after your station! You know when to get ready to get off the train (or bus).
5 On the Trans-Siberian Railroad, bring lots of food and drink with you! The people on the train like to share. Extra food you have helps you meet and speak with new people on the train.
6 Learn a few words in the local language. This can help when asking for directions, buying tickets or asking where to get off the bus.

confusing – verwirrend; **possible** – mögliche; **a few** – einige; **destination** – Ziel (einer Fahrt); **piece of paper** – Blatt Papier; **don't be afraid** – keine Angst haben; **ask directions** – nach dem Weg fragen; **(to) get lost** – verloren gehen; **local** – Einheimischer; **(to) get ready** – bereit machen; **local language** – Landessprache; **(to) get off (the bus)** – aussteigen (aus dem Bus)

G Grammar

1 Das Verb

1.1 Das Verb *to be*

Formen					
bejaht		verneint		im Fragesatz	
Langform	Kurzform	Langform	Kurzform	bejaht	verneint
I am	*I'm*	*I am not*	*I'm not*	*am I?*	*am I not?*
you are	*you're*	*you are not*	*you aren't / you're not*	*are you?*	*aren't you?*
he is *she is* *it is*	*he's* *she's* *it's*	*he is not* *she is not* *it is not*	*he isn't / he's not* *she isn't / she's not* *it isn't / it's not*	*is he?* *is she?* *is it?*	*isn't he?* *isn't she?* *isn't it?*
we are	*we're*	*we are not*	*we aren't / we're not*	*are we*	*aren't we?*
you are	*you're*	*you are not*	*you aren't / you're not*	*are you?*	*aren't you?*
they are	*they're*	*they are not*	*they aren't / they're not*	*are they?*	*aren't they?*

- to be wird benutzt, um zu sagen oder zu fragen, wer man ist, woher man kommt und welche Nationalität man hat:
  I am Peter. / I'm Peter.
  You are Sarah. / You're Sarah.
  Are you Harry?
  Are you from Liverpool?
  Are you from here?
  Where are you from?
  Are you English?
  Yes, I am. / No, I'm not. I'm Irish. I'm from Ireland.
- Mit to be wird auch einfach gesagt, was etwas ist:
  This is a book. This is a bag. This is a pencil.
- Bei Fragen wird to be an den Anfang der Frage gestellt:
  Is it a cinema? *Yes, it is. It's a cinema.*
  Is it a hotel? *No, it's not. / No, it isn't.*
- Um zu sagen, wo sich jemand oder etwas befindet, wird ebenfalls to be verwendet:
  Angela is in the theatre.
  Bill is in the museum.
  John is in the cathedral.
  Is the hotel in London?
  No, it's not / No, it isn't. It's in Moscow.
  They aren't in the restaurant.
  They are in Market Street.
- Mit there is/there are wird das Verb to be verwendet, um auszudrücken, dass es etwas gibt:
  There is a bank.
  There are lots of restaurants.
  Is there a post office near here?
  Yes, there is. / No, there isn't.

1.2 Die einfache Gegenwart (*simple present*)

Formen			
im Aussagesatz		im Fragesatz	
bejaht	verneint	bejaht	verneint
I read	*I don't read*	*do I read?*	*don't I read?*
you read	*you don't read*	*do you read?*	*don't you read?*
he reads *she reads* *it reads*	*he doesn't read* *she doesn't read* *it doesn't read*	*does he read?* *does she read?* *does it read?*	*doesn't he read?* *doesn't she read?* *doesn't it read?*
we read	*we don't read*	*do we read?*	*don't we read?*
you read	*you don't read*	*do you read?*	*don't you read?*
they read	*they don't read*	*do they read?*	*don't they read?*

- Bei he/she/it wird in bejahten Aussagesätzen -s an das Verb angehängt:
  I read a book. – He reads a book.
  I listen to music. – He listens to music.
- Einige Verben haben bei he/she/it eine Sonderform:
  I go to work. – He goes to work.
  I have a shower. – She has a shower.

- Fragen und verneinte Formen werden mit do/does bzw. don't/doesn't gebildet:
  I don't like classical music.
  Do you like pop music? No, I don't.
  Does Sam like cheese?
  No, he doesn't. He doesn't eat cheese.
  Luke doesn't eat meat.
  He's a vegetarian and vegetarians don't eat meat.
  What does 'Senf' mean? – It means 'mustard'.
- Bei Antworten auf eine Frage mit do/does wird oft auch in der bejahten Form do/does wiederholt:
  Do you live in Germany? Yes, I do.
  Does paella have meat in it? Yes, it does.

1.3 *have (got)*

- Um zu sagen, dass man etwas ‚hat' bzw. ‚besitzt', wird have benutzt:
  I have a car. *He has a dog.*
- Daneben gibt es auch den Ausdruck have got/has got (Kurzform: 've got/'s got):
  I've got a computer in my bedroom.
  I haven't got a TV.
  The house has got two bedrooms.
- In Fragen wird have/has vorangestellt:
  Have you got a garden? – Yes, I have. / No, I haven't.

1.4 *can*

- Das Modalverb can (verneint: can't) entspricht dem deutschen ‚können' und wird mit einem anderen Verb zusammen verwendet. Wie alle Hilfs- und Modalverben kann es bei der Verneinung oder in Fragen nicht mit do/does kombiniert werden:
  I can ski. – Can you?
  Can you speak Japanese? – No, I can't.

2 Artikel und Substantive

2.1 Die Artikel *a* und *the*

- Wenn man etwas im Gespräch erstmals erwähnt, verwendet man den unbestimmten Artikel a vor einem Substantiv. Er kann nur mit zählbaren Substantiven im Singular stehen:
  a museum, a cinema, a restaurant, a newspaper
- Wenn man sich auf etwas Bestimmtes oder Bekanntes beziehen will, z.B. was im Gespräch schon erwähnt wurde oder was allgemein bekannt ist, wird im Englischen der bestimmte Artikel the verwendet, der vor Substantiven in der Ein- und Mehrzahl stehen kann:
  the Louvre, the Eiffel Tower, the Ritz
  the cars, the books

2.2 Das Substantiv

- Um die Mehrzahl eines Substantivs im Englischen zu bilden, wird regelmäßig ein s an die Einzahl angehängt:
  I have two cars.
  I speak three languages.
  We are ten students.
  I work eight hours a day.
  I live 20 kilometres from Munich.
- Um sich auf eine unbestimmte Menge in der Mehrzahl beziehen (‚einige'), so wird die Mengenbezeichnung some verwendet:
  some shoes, some newspapers
- Einige Substantive haben unregelmäßige Mehrzahlformen:
  one child – two children
  one man – two men
  one woman – two women
- Die Genitivendung eines Substantivs lautet 's, und wird mit einem Apostroph geschrieben. Das Genitiv s wird sehr häufig bei Namen verwendet:
  June is Sally's mother.
  Tammy is Claire's daughter.
  This is a photo of Gary's family.

3 Pronomen

3.1 Besitzanzeigende Fürwörter

- Für die Besitzanzeige werden im Englischen Fürwörter verwendet, die immer vor dem Substantiv stehen:

Formen	
I	*my*
you	*your*
he *she* *it*	*his* *her* *its*
we	*our*
you	*your*
they	*their*

This is my bag.
This is your car.
This is his briefcase.
This is her handbag.
This is a photo of our class.
Where are their children?

- Mit dem Pronomen this verweist man auf ganz bestimmte Dinge:
  This is my house. *This is my handbag.*

3.2 Fragefürwörter

- Mit den Fragefürwörtern where, what, how und how many werden Fragen gebildet. Die Fragefürwörter stehen immer vor dem Verb:
  Where are you from?
  What do you want?
  How do you feel?
  How many books have you got at home?
  How many people are in the class?

4 Adverbien

- Mit Adverbien können Verben oder Adjektive näher bestimmt werden. Mit Häufigkeitsadverbien wird ausgesagt, wie oft etwas getan wird. Sie stehen meistens vor dem Verb:
  My family and I always go to France on holiday.
  We never fly – we normally drive, but sometimes we take the train.

K Homestudy – Answer key

Unit 1

1
1 Egypt, Egyptian
2 Germany, German
3 Mongolia, Mongolian
4 England, English
5 America, American
6 Asia, Asian
7 Denmark, Danish
8 Switzerland, Swiss

2
1 Japan
2 New Zealand
3 Spain
4 Colombia
5 Morocco
6 Peru

3
1 Japan is not in Europe. It's in Asia.
2 New Zealand is in Australasia. It's not in Africa.
3 Spain is not in Asia. It's in Europe.
4 Colombia is not in North America. It's in South America.
5 Morocco is not in South America. It's in Africa.
6 Peru is not in Australasia. It's in South America.

4
1 Hitomi Kitano 2 Larry Lewis
3 Monika Czarnok 4 Mauro Varese
5 Maria Varese 6 Urs Müller

5
1 E 2 A 3 C 4 D 5 B

6
1 friend 2 class 3 meet 4 house
5 France

7
Across:
4 chocolate
6 house
8 pizza
10 taxi
11 beer

Down:
1 coffee
2 garden
3 tea
5 music
7 water
9 wine

Unit 2

1
1 It's a plane.
2 It's a lounge.
3 It's a boarding card.
4 It's a café.
5 It's a restaurant.
6 It's a car park.

2

Name:	Angela Smith
Flight Time:	12.30
Destination:	Munich
Gate:	15

3
1 are 2 are 3 is 4 is 5 isn't
6 are 7 aren't 8 isn't

4
1 Yes, she is.
2 No it isn't. It's in London.
3 Yes, it is.
4 No, they're not./aren't.
5 Yes, they are.

5
1 D 2 C 3 A 4 E 5 B

6
1 Where is Disneyland?
2 Where is the Eiffel Tower?
3 Where is the Red Square?
4 Where is the 'Reichstag'?
5 Where is the Golden Gate Bridge?

7
1 Disneyland is in California.
2 The Eiffel Tower is in Paris.
3 The Red Square is in Moscow
4 The 'Reichstag' is in Berlin.
5 The Golden Gate Bridge is in San Francisco.

8
1 Notre Dame is a Cathedral
2 London is a city in England. It's the capital of England.
3 My car is in the car park here.
4 Bill isn't a German name.
5 La Scala isn't a cinema. It's the name of the Opera House in Milan.
6 My name is Angelique. It's a French name.

9
1 eleven 2 twenty-eight 3 seventeen

10
1 thirty 2 fifteen 3 thirteen
4 eighty-six 5 ninety-four

Unit 3

1
1 coffee, tea 2 beer, wine 3 football, tennis

2
1 watch 2 read 3 listen 4 play
5 have 6 phone

3
1 goes to work in the morning.
2 likes books and reads a lot.
3 speaks a little English.
4 watches TV in the evening.
5 plays football on Sunday.
6 lives in Berlin.

4
1 boy, girls
2 cars
3 students
4 languages
5 cities

5

1 Can you speak English?	Yes, I can.
2 Can you drive?	No, I can't.
3 Can you ski?	Yes, I can.
4 Can you cook spaghetti?	Yes, I can.
5 Can you swim?	No, I can't.
6 Can you play cricket?	No, I can't.

6
1 Mandy 2 Greg 3 Greg
4 Mandy 5 Mandy 6 Greg
7 Greg 8 Greg 9 Mandy 10 Mandy

7
1 Yes, I do.
2 I go there in summer.
3 I go to Rimini or Venice.
4 I can speak a little Italian.
5 Yes, I do.
6 Yes, I do.

Unit 4

1
1 curry and rice **2** pizza, spaghetti **3** fruit salad **4** paella **5** burger, spaghetti, chips **6** spaghetti

2
1 waiter **2** customer **3** waiter **4** customer **5** customer **6** waiter **7** waiter **8** customer **9** customer **10** waiter

3
1 D **2** H **3** A **4** E **5** G **6** B **7** F **8** C

4
1 fruit juice **2** grapes **3** lamb **4** lettuce **5** chips

5
Len: Spaghetti, mineral water, Italian wine
Alice: Fish with salad

6
1 ✗ You can get meat from a butcher.
2 ✓
3 ✓
4 ✗ You can get newspapers from a newsagent.
5 ✓
6 ✗ You can get aspirin from a chemist.

7
1 F **2** D **3** E **4** B **5** A **6** C

Unit 5

1
1 toilet **2** cooker **3** shower **4** washing **5** fridge **6** sofa

2
1 Have **2** Do **3** How **4** Where **5** Do **6** Have

3
1 animals **2** What's, father's **3** sisters **4** Where's, Jack's **5** friends, hours

4
1 D **2** H **3** G **4** E **5** F **6** A **7** B **8** C

5
Don and June have: tickets, money, laptop, keys, tissues, glasses
Don and June don't have: passport

6
1 E **2** C **3** B **4** D **5** A

7
1 Your mother
2 Your grandparents
3 Your grandchildren
4 Your parents
5 You, your brothers and sisters
6 Your sister

8
1 E **2** G **3** F **4** A **5** D **6** C **7** B

Transcripts

Unit 1 A

2
Track 1.2

1 tea
2 wine
3 house
4 beer
5 music
6 chocolate
7 pizza
8 coffee
9 water
10 garden
11 taxi

3
Track 1.3

Pete Hello, I'm Pete.
Jane Hello. I'm Jane.

4
Track 1.4

Pete Jane?
Jane Yes?
Pete OK … the party.
Jane OK.
Pete Wine?
Jane Yes.
Pete Beer?
Jane Yes. And pizza.
Pete Yes, pizza. Spaghetti?
Jane No, no spaghetti!
Pete OK, OK, no spaghetti. Whisky and ice?
Jane Umm … OK.
Pete OK. Tea and coffee?
Jane Umm. Tea – no. Coffee.
Pete OK – no tea. Coffee, yes. Water?
Jane Yes, water. And … chocolate.
Pete Chocolate? No.
Jane No? …
Pete OK, chocolate.
Jane Good. Thanks.

5
Track 1.5

Jane Hello.
Max Hi. I'm Max.
Jane Hi. Nice to meet you. I'm Jane.
Max Hi. And this is Fran.
Jane Hi Fran.
Fran Hello. Nice to meet you, Jane.
Jane Pete – Max and Fran.
Pete Hi Max.
Max Hi Pete. This is Fran.
Fran Hello. Nice to meet you.
Pete Nice to meet you, too.

Unit 1 B

2
Track 1.6

Sarah Hello.
Andreas Hello. Good afternoon.
Sarah I'm here for a car.
Andreas OK. Are you Ms Smith?
Sarah No, I'm not.
Andreas No. You're Ms …?
Sarah Ms Jackson.
Andreas Ah, Ms Jackson. From Birmingham?
Sarah Yes, I'm from Birmingham.

3
Track 1.7

Andreas Hello.
Dennis Hello.
Andreas How can I help you?
Dennis I'm here for my BMW.
Andreas OK. What's your name?
Dennis Smith. Mr Smith.
Andreas Are you Mr D. Smith?
Dennis Yes.
Andreas Here you are. Mr David Smith from Liverpool.
Dennis No, I'm Dennis, not David. And I'm not from Liverpool.
Andreas Oh. You're Dennis. Are you from Manchester?
Dennis Yes, I'm from Manchester.
Andreas OK. Yes.

6
Track 1.8

1 c-a-r
2 a-p-p-l-e
3 c-o-f-f-e-e
4 c-h-o-c-o-l-a-t-e
5 s-p-a-g-h-e-t-t-i
6 w-a-t-e-r
7 p-a-s-t-a
8 h-o-u-s-e

Unit 1 C

4 Track 1.9

1 Hi. I'm Japanese.
2 I'm from Los Angeles.
3 I'm not Swiss. I'm American. Polish-American.
4 I'm from Milano – Milan in English.
5 You're from Nagasaki? I'm from Italy.
6 I'm from Zug in Switzerland.

Unit 2 A

3 Track 1.10

1 WM 53 CED
2 EY 21 FGP
3 SZ 82 UQO

4 Track 1.11

Jane Hi Simon. How are you?
Simon Hi Jane. Fine, thanks.
Jane Good. Simon, is this your mobile number? 07964 823519?
Simon No, it's not. My number is 07955 681243.
Jane Ah! Good. 1234
Simon No, 1243.
Jane Ah, OK. 1243.
Simon And what's your number?
Jane 08873 462915
Simon Right. Thanks.

Unit 2 B

2 Track 1.12

1 19 99
2 It's 11 45
3 It's 20 12
4 Jane is 58.

4 Track 1.13

Louise Hi everyone. Good morning. I'm Louise and I'm your guide today. Right.
Bill Is this a museum?
Louise No, it's not a museum. This is a cathedral. The Cathedral of Saint John. Twenty minutes here.

Bill Excuse me?
Louise Yes?
Bill What's this?
Louise This is the City Museum. It's interesting. Forty minutes here, OK?

Bill What's this? Is it a cinema?
Louise No, it's not a cinema. OK everyone. Now this is the theatre. It's famous.
Hee-Jun Theatre?
Louise Yes, Shakespeare, Molière, Brecht, you know. Thirty minutes here.

Louise Hello again. Now, it's one ten. This is the restaurant. Fifty minutes here.

Hee-Jun Excuse me?
Louise Yes?
Hee-Jun What's this street?
Louise This is Market Street – shops, shops, shops. Sixty minutes – one hour – here. OK?
Bill Ah, shopping. Fantastic.

Unit 2 C

2 Track 1.14

Angela Oh, no.
Bill What?
Angela Look. My boarding card is wrong.
Bill What's wrong?
Angela Here – my name's not Schmidt. It's Smith. I'm not German …
Bill Oh. Right. I see.
Angela And the time. It's not 11.45.
Bill Yes. You're right. That's wrong. It's 12.30. 12.30 to Munich.
Angela Yes, 12.30. 11.45 isn't right.
Bill Oh – and look! The seat number. You're in seat 14C
Angela And you? What's your seat number?
Bill I'm in 24D.
Angela Oh, no. That's wrong too. And the gate number?
Bill Gate 15.
Angela 50?
Bill No, gate 15 …
Angela Oh. That's right. Wrong seat, wrong name, wrong time, right gate.

Transcripts

Unit 3 A

5 Track 1.15

Sue Hi Mark.
Mark Hi Sue.
Sue Tell me about a normal day.
Mark OK. Well, in the morning I have a shower, and I go to work.
Sue OK. And in the afternoon?
Mark Right. I have a sandwich or a pizza. I like pizza.
Sue Really? I don't. OK.
Mark And I work. I use my computer.
Sue I see. And in the evening?
Mark I watch TV. And I listen to music.
Sue What music? Classical?
Mark No. I don't like classical music. I listen to rock music.
Sue I don't like that. I like punk.
Mark Punk! That's not music!

Unit 3 B

9 Track 1.16

Bob Do you like sport, John?
John Yes, I do. Not football – but rugby.
Bob You don't like football? Really? It's my favourite sport.
John No. I play rugby. And golf and cricket.
Bob That's a lot. For me, it's football.
John Do you play a lot?
Bob No, I don't play. I watch it on TV. With a beer.
John I see. I don't drink. Not beer or wine.
Bob I swim a little.
John I can't swim.
Bob Really? You can't swim?
John No.
Bob It's great. We go to Spain in the summer.
John Spain? Can you speak Spanish?
Bob Yes, a little.

Unit 3 C

7 Track 1.17

Franco Excuse me.
Anne Yes?
Franco Can I ask you two or three questions, please?
Anne OK.
Franco OK. Do you know Italy?
Anne Yes. I do. I go there in the summer.
Franco Where do you go?
Anne I go to Rimini or Venice.
Franco Right. Good. Can you speak Italian?
Anne I can speak a little Italian.
Franco Right. Very good. Do you watch Italian films?
Anne Yes, I do. I like them.
Franco Where do you watch them? On TV?
Anne Yes, on TV, and I go to the cinema with my friend.
Franco Good. Good. Very good. Do you like Italian food?
Anne Yes, I do.
Franco Do you have Italian friends?
Anne Yes. I do.
Franco Oh. I see.

Unit 4 A

5 Track 1.18

1
Carl Hello. Good evening. I'm Carl, and I'm your waiter today. Here's the menu.
Tina Thank you.
Carl Can I get you a drink?
Tina Yes, please. A white wine for me, please.
Carl Yes, and for you, sir?
Phil A beer, please.
Carl Right.
(Pause)
Carl OK. A white wine and a beer. Here you are.
Tina/Phil Thanks.

2
Waitress Hello. What would you like?
Pete Hmmn. I'm not sure.
Lucy The paella is very good.
Pete What's in it?
Waitress Rice and fish.
Lucy Oh – he doesn't eat fish.
Waitress I see.
Pete OK. Curry for me, please.
Lucy And paella for me.
Waitress Right. And to drink? Coke? Wine? Beer?
Pete Just water, please. Mineral water.

Unit 4 B

2 + 3 Track 1.19

1

Jane	Excuse me?
Matt	Yes?
Jane	What's your name, please?
Matt	Matt. Matt Frye.
Jane	Matt, do you like shopping?
Matt	I love shopping.
Jane	Really? Shopping for what?
Matt	For shoes, for books, for clothes.
Jane	For food?
Matt	No. My wife does that. I hate supermarkets.

2

Jane	And your name is …?
Sally	Sally.
Jane	Sally, do you like shopping?
Sally	No, I don't.
Jane	Really?
Sally	Yes. I hate shopping. Oh – but shopping for music is OK. I love music.
Jane	Ah. Do you have a favourite shop?
Sally	No. I shop online.

3

Jane	Vic, do you have a favourite shop?
Vic	Well, yes. The travel agent.
Jane	Why?
Vic	I love holidays!

Unit 4 C

5 Track 1.20

Len	Excuse me, I think we are ready. Can we order?
Waiter	No problem. What would you like?
Alice	For me, the chicken, please.
Waiter	Chicken. With chips?
Alice	Yes. No – with salad, please.
Waiter	OK. And for you?
Alice	Oh – no. Do you have paella?
Waiter	Sorry, no paella, not today … we have fish.
Alice	Good idea. Fish for me, please.
Waiter	With chips?
Alice	No, with salad, please.
Waiter	Right.
Len	And for me, let's see … kebabs, no, burger …
Waiter	The pork is very good
Len	No, no thanks … spaghetti or pizza. Spaghetti, I think.
Waiter	Right. Thank you. And drinks?
Len	Yes, some mineral water, and … wine, Italian wine, I think, please.
Waiter	Certainly.

Unit 5 A

5 Track 1.21

1

Jane	Tell me, Nick – what's your favourite room at home?
Nick	That's a good question. My favourite room is … not a room. It's the garden.
Jane	Oh.
Nick	Yes. I love the garden. It's not big, but I love it. Really.
Jane	I see.
Nick	And what about you? What's your favourite room at home?
Jane	Easy – my bedroom.
Nick	Not the kitchen or living room?
Jane	No. I cook in the kitchen, and I don't like that. The living room is OK, but my favourite room is my bedroom.
Nick	Why?
Jane	It's big, I love my bed, and I've got a TV there. It's a lovely room.

2

Jane	Do you live in a house or a flat, Max?
Max	No, I don't.
Jane	No? Where do you live? In a park?
Max	No. I live in a hotel.
Jane	In a hotel? Why?
Max	I love it. The rooms are nice. It's in the centre of the city, I don't cook – there are two restaurants in the hotel, and the hotel has got a swimming pool and a gym.
Jane	Wow!
Max	Yes. Money is not a problem for me, so the hotel is my home.

Transcripts

Unit 5 B

5 Track 1.22

1

Rob I've got a lovely photo of my mother. Here she is.

Jill How old's your mum?

Rob Now, my mum is 78, but in this photo she is 25 or 26. She is young.

Jill Lovely photo.

Rob And she's with her dog, Judy. This is before I was born.

Jill Has she got a dog now?

Rob No, she hasn't. I like this photo because she is young and happy. My mum, not the dog.

2

Nina Who's this in the photo?

Billy Me.

Nina You, Billy? Really!

Billy Yes. This is me in 1982.

Nina Wow. You've got long hair

Billy Yes.

Nina I've got a photo of me. And that's Mike.

Billy Is he your boyfriend?

Nina No. He's my big brother! Mike and his lovely sister Nina.

Billy Oh?

Nina He's 48.

Billy Oh, right.

Unit 5 C

5 Track 1.23

June Is the taxi here?

Don Yes. So, have you got the tickets for the plane?

June Tickets … yes, here in my bag.

Don Good. And you've got the address of the hotel?

June Yes. Here.

Don Glasses? Money? Laptop? You've got them?

June Yes, yes … laptop, yes.

Don Where are the keys?

June Here, got them. Got tissues – here you are.

Don Thanks.

June So, we're ready?

Don Great. We can go.

June Good. You've got your passport?

Don Passport, passport? No, where's my passport? Where's my passport? You haven't got it?

June Oh, Don!

Unit 6 A

6 Track 1.24

Kelly Tomorrow is the start of our holiday.

Jo Really? Lucky you.

Kelly Yes.

Jo So, what's your plan?

Kelly Well, the plane leaves at 7 in the evening.

Jo OK.

Kelly But that's from London.

Jo Heathrow ?

Kelly Yes. So, first we take a taxi from here to the station. Then we go to London by train. Then in London we take the underground to Heathrow. That takes about an hour, I think.

Jo So then you fly, and that's it.

Kelly Yes and no. Then we fly to Rome, but that's not it.

Jo No?

Kelly No. We are in Rome for two days, then we get a car and drive to the south. Then we take the boat to Sicily. And that's it.

Jo Wow. Interesting.

Unit 6 B

6 Track 1.25

1

Alison We don't have a lot of money, so we can't have expensive holidays with hotels and things. But we love the sun. So, normally we go camping somewhere warm. We know some great places in France.

2

Ian My wife's favourite place is Paris – the restaurants, the shops, the culture. Two or three days of that and she is happy. I don't really like big cities. So many people, and noise. I prefer nature. A week of skiing in the mountains of Switzerland, that's my perfect holiday.

3

Marie I don't like shopping, and I don't like museums. For me, the perfect holiday is two weeks on a beach somewhere hot. Greece, Turkey, Spain and Italy are fantastic.

CD

Track	Unit	Part	Exercise	Running time
1.1			Copyright & credits	0:44
1.2	1	A	Exercise 2	0:54
1.3		A	Exercise 3	0:10
1.4		A	Exercise 4	1:02
1.5		A	Exercise 5	0:36
1.6		B	Exercise 2	0:29
1.7		B	Exercise 3	0:44
1.8		B	Exercise 6	1:39
1.9		C	Exercise 4	0:46
1.10	2	A	Exercise 3	0:45
1.11		A	Exercise 4	1:18
1.12		B	Exercise 2	0:28
1.13		B	Exercise 4	1:58
1.14		C	Exercise 2	1:21
1.15	3	A	Exercise 5	1:01
1.16		B	Exercise 9	1:04
1.17		C	Exercise 7	1:14
1.18	4	A	Exercise 5	1:15
1.19		B	Exercise 2 + 3	1:19
1.20		C	Exercise 5	1:09
1.21	5	A	Exercise 5	1:44
1.22		B	Exercise 5	1:13
1.23		C	Exercise 5	0:57
1.24	6	A	Exercise 6	1:08
1.25		B	Exercise 6	1:09
			Total running time	**25:55**

Aufnahmeleitung:
James Richardson

Toningeneur:
Darrin Brown

Tontechnik:
The Soundhouse, London

Verlagsredaktion:
Martin Maier

Sprecher/innen:
Alison Dowling
Ben Elliot
DeNica Fairman
Rob Fitch
Harriet Kershaw
Roger May
David Thorpe
Joan Walker

Unit word list

Verwendete Abkürzungen

jdm	jemandem
jdn	jemanden
sb	somebody
sth	something
s.o.	someone
etw	etwas

Hinweise zur Aussprache

ɑ: wie in car [kɑ:]
ʌ wie in bus [bʌs]
æ wie in can [kæn]
e wie in yes [jes]
i: wie in he [hi:]
i wie in happy ['hæpi]
ɪ wie in it [ɪt]
ɜ: wie in birthday ['bɜ:θdeɪ]
ɒ wie in watch [wɒtʃ]
ɔ: wie in short [ʃɔ:t]
ʊ wie in book [bʊk]
u: wie in food [fu:d]
u wie in January ['dʒænjuəri]
ə wie in father ['fɑ:ðə]
aɪ wie in flight ['flaɪt]
aʊ wie in house [haʊs]
eɪ wie in name [neɪm]
ɔɪ wie in boy [bɔɪ]
ɪə wie in hear [hɪə]
eə wie in hair [heə]
əʊ wie in phone [fəʊn]
ʊə wie in sure [ʃʊə]
ŋ wie in living ['lɪvɪŋ]
s wie in sorry ['sɒri]
z wie in easy ['i:zi]
ʃ wie in shop [ʃɒp]
tʃ wie in chicken ['tʃɪkɪn]
dʒ wie in just [dʒʌst]
v wie in visit ['vɪzɪt]
r wie in rain [reɪn]
ʒ wie in television ['telɪvɪʒn]
θ wie in theatre ['θɪətə]
ð wie in other ['ʌðə]
w wie in wonderful ['wʌndəfʊl]

Unit 01, Part A

hello	[hə'ləʊ]	hallo
I	[aɪ]	ich
am	[em]	bin
I'm	[aɪm]	ich bin

1

how	[haʊ]	wie
are	[ɑ:]	bist, sind, seid
you	[ju:]	du, ihr, Sie
How are you?	[ˌhaʊ ə 'ju:]	Wie geht es dir/euch/Ihnen?

2

chocolate	['tʃɒklət]	Schokolade, Praline
tea	[ti:]	Tee
coffee	['kɒfi]	Kaffee
wine	[waɪn]	Wein
beer	[bɪə]	Bier
house	[haʊs]	Haus
music	['mju:zɪk]	Musik
garden	['gɑ:dn]	Garten
water	['wɔ:tə]	Wasser
taxi	['tæksi]	Taxi

4

apple	['æpl]	Apfel
car	[kɑ:]	Auto
fruit	[fru:t]	Obst, Frucht, Früchte
place	[pleɪs]	Ort, Platz, Zuhause
whisky	['wiski]	Whiskey

5

nice	[naɪs]	nett, hübsch, schön
to **meet** sb	[mi:t]	jdm begegnen
Nice to meet you.	[ˌnaɪs tə 'mi:t ju]	Schön, dich/Sie kennen zu lernen.
is	[ɪz]	ist
… , **too**	[tu:]	auch, ebenso

7

my	[maɪ]	mein
object	['ɒbdʒɪkt]	Gegenstand
pen	[pen]	Stift
class	[klɑ:s]	Kurs
book	[bʊk]	Buch
chair	[tʃeə]	Stuhl

9

Take care.	[ˌteɪk 'keə]	Pass auf dich/Passen Sie auf sich auf.
Goodbye.	[ˌgʊd'baɪ]	Auf Wiedersehen.
bye	[baɪ]	tschüs
good	[gʊd]	gut
thanks	[θæŋks]	danke

Unit 01, Part B

1

here	[hɪə]	hier

2

car hire	['kɑ: haɪə]	Autovermietung
office	['ɒfɪs]	Büro
Ms	[mɪz]	Frau

2 **1.6**

afternoon	[ˌɑ:ftə'nu:n]	Nachmittag
for	[fə]	für
Birmingham	['bɜ:mɪŋəm]	*Stadt in Mittelengland*

3

family	['fæməli]	Familie
family name	['fæməli neɪm]	Familienname
first name	['fɜ:st neɪm]	Vorname
city	['sɪti]	Stadt
to **keep**	[ki:p]	behalten
copy	['kɒpi]	Exemplar, Kopie
records	['rekɔ:dz]	Unterlagen
to **help**	[help]	helfen
Mr	['mɪstə]	Herr
yes	[jes]	ja
Here you are.	[ˌhɪə ju 'ɑ:]	Bitte sehr.
Liverpool	['lɪvəpu:l]	*Stadt in Nordwestengland*
no	[nəʊ]	nein
Manchester	['mæntʃɪstə]	*Stadt in Nordwestengland*

4

Spain	[speɪn]	Spanien
Bulgaria	[bʌl'geəriə]	Bulgarien
German	['dʒɜ:mən]	deutsch
Croatian	[krəʊ'eɪʃən]	kroatisch
American	[ə'merɪkən]	amerikanisch
French	[frentʃ]	französisch
Polish	['pəlɪʃ]	polnisch

Switzerland	['swɪtsələnd]	Schweiz
country	['kʌntri]	Land
nationality	[ˌnæʃə'næləti]	Staatsangehörigkeit
England	['ɪŋglənd]	England
France	[frɑːns]	Frankreich
Spanish	['spænɪʃ]	spanisch
Germany	['dʒɜːməni]	Deutschland
Italian	[ɪ'tæljən]	italienisch
Poland	['pəʊlənd]	Polen
America	[ə'merɪkə]	Amerika
the United States	[ðə juˌnaɪtɪd 'steɪts]	die Vereinigten Staaten
Swiss	[swɪs]	schweizerisch
Croatia	[krəʊ'eɪʃə]	Kroatien
Bulgarian	[bʌl'geəriən]	bulgarisch

6

letter	['letə]	Buchstabe

7

street	[striːt]	Straße
favourite	['feɪvərɪt]	Lieblings-
lesson	['lesn]	(Unterrichts-)Stunde

Unit 01, Part C

1

Genghis Khan	[ˌdʒeŋgɪs 'kɑːn]	Dschingis Khan *(mongolischer Herrscher)*
Mongolia	[mɒŋ'gəʊliə]	Mongolei
William Tell	[ˌwɪljəm 'tel]	Wilhelm Tell *(schweizer Nationalheld)*
little	['lɪtl]	klein
mermaid	['mɜːmeɪd]	Meerjungfrau
The Little Mermaid	[ðə ˌlɪtl 'mɜːmeɪd]	Die kleine Meerjungfrau *(Märchenfigur nach Hans Christian Andersen)*

2

continent	['kɒntɪnənt]	Kontinent
Europe	['jʊərəp]	Europa
Africa	['æfrɪkə]	Afrika
Asia	['eɪʃə]	Asien
North America	[ˌnɔːθ ə'merɪkə]	Nordamerika
South America	[ˌsaʊθ ə'merɪkə]	Südamerika
Australasia	[ˌɒstrə'leɪʃə]	Australien, Neuseeland und Ozeanien
South Africa	[ˌsaʊθ 'æfrɪkə]	Südafrika
Canada	['kænədə]	Kanada
Argentina	[ˌɑːdʒən'tiːnə]	Argentinien
Australia	[ɒ'streɪliə]	Australien
Tunisia	[tju'nɪziə]	Tunesien
India	['ɪndiə]	Indien
Colombia	[kə'lɒmbiə]	Kolumbien
Brazil	[brə'zɪl]	Brasilien
Japan	[dʒə'pæn]	Japan
New Zealand	[ˌnjuː 'ziːlənd]	Neuseeland
Morocco	[mə'rɒkəʊ]	Marokko

3

Asian	['eɪʃn]	asiatisch
South American	[ˌsaʊθ ə'merɪkən]	südamerikanisch

4

female	['fiːmeɪl]	weiblich
Japanese	[ˌdʒæpə'niːz]	japanisch

5

China	['tʃaɪnə]	China
Chinese	[tʃaɪ'niːz]	chinesisch, Chinese, Chinesin

Unit 02, Part A

1

Rome	[rəʊm]	Rom
Moscow	['mɒskəʊ]	Moskau
Lisbon	['lɪzbən]	Lissabon
Colosseum	[ˌkɒlə'siəm]	Kolosseum
tower	['taʊə]	Turm
The Eiffel Tower	[ðiː ˌaɪfl 'taʊə]	der Eiffelturm *(in Paris)*
opera	['ɒprə]	Oper
white	[waɪt]	weiß
the White House	[ðə 'waɪt haʊs]	das Weiße Haus *(in Washington)*
red	[red]	rot
square	[skweə]	Platz
The Red Square	[ðə red 'skweə]	der Rote Platz *(in Moskau)*

4

telephone	['telɪfəʊn]	Telefon
to **count**	[kaʊnt]	zählen
counting number	['kaʊntɪŋ nʌmbə]	Nummern (auf-)zählen

5

cinema	['sɪnəmə]	Kino
school	[skuːl]	Schule
restaurant	['restrɒnt]	Restaurant
hotel	[həʊ'tel]	Hotel
pub	[pʌb]	Kneipe
theatre	['θɪətə]	Theater
cathedral	[kə'θiːdrəl]	Dom, Kathedrale
museum	[mju'ziːəm]	Museum
it	[ɪt]	es

7

address	[ə'dres]	Adresse
mobile	['məʊbaɪl]	Handy, Mobiltelefon

8

phone number	['fəʊn nʌmbə]	Telefonnummer

Unit 02, Part B

3

was born	[wɒz bɔːn]	geboren (sein)
now	[naʊ]	jetzt

4

city tour	['sɪti tʊə]	Stadtrundfahrt
to **visit**	['vɪzɪt]	besuchen, besichtigen
minute	['mɪnɪt]	Minute
Saint John	[seɪnt 'dʒɒn]	hl. Johannes

4 **1.13**

everyone	['evriwʌn]	jede/r/s
guide	[gaɪd]	Reiseführer/-in
today	[tə'deɪ]	heute
to **excuse (s.o.)**	[ɪk'skjuːs]	(jdn) entschuldigen
Excuse me.	[ɪk'skjuːz mi]	Entschuldigung./ Verzeihung.
interesting	['ɪntrəstɪŋ]	interessant
famous	['feɪməs]	berühmt
to **know**	[nəʊ]	wissen, kennen
again	[ə'gen]	wieder
shopping	['ʃɒpɪŋ]	Einkaufen
fantastic	[fæn'tæstɪk]	fantastisch

5

where	[weə]	wo
to **choose**	[tʃuːz]	wählen
different	['dɪfrənt]	andere/r/s, unterschiedliche/r/s
time	[taɪm]	Zeit

U Unit word list

7

true	[tru:]	richtig, wahr
false	[fɔ:ls]	falsch
Edinburgh	['edɪnbərə]	*Hauptstadt Schottlands*
Glasgow	['glɑ:sgəʊ]	*größte Stadt Schottlands*
teacher	['ti:tʃə]	Leherer/in
friend	[frend]	Freund/in

Unit 02, Part C

1

boarding card	['bɔ:dɪŋ kɑ:d]	Bordkarte
café	['kæfeɪ]	Café
car park	['kɑ: pɑ:k]	Parkplatz, Parkhaus, Tiefgarage
lounge	[laʊndʒ]	Wartesaal, -halle
plane	[pleɪn]	Flugzeug

2

flight	[flaɪt]	Flug
destination	[ˌdestɪ'neɪʃn]	Zielort, Bestimmungsort
Munich	['mju:nɪk]	München
gate	[geɪt]	Tor, *hier:* Flugsteig
seat	[si:t]	Sitz, Platz

2 **1.14**

to **see**	[si:]	*hier:* verstehen

3

airport	['eəpɔ:t]	Flughafen

4

British	['brɪtɪʃ]	britisch
Milan	[mɪ'læn]	Mailand

6

bridge	[brɪdʒ]	Brücke

8

gap	[gæp]	Lücke
capital	['kæpɪtl]	Hauptstadt
opera house	['ɒprə haʊs]	Opernhaus

Unit 03, Part A

to **like sth**	[laɪk]	etwas mögen

1

football	['fʊtbɔ:l]	Fußball
tennis	['tenɪs]	Tennis
to **add**	[æd]	hinzufügen
activity	[æk'tɪvəti]	Tätigkeit, Aktivität
interest	['ɪntrəst]	Interesse
sports	[spɔ:ts]	Sport
classical	['klæsɪkl]	klassisch
food	[fu:d]	Essen
drink	[drɪŋk]	Getränk
mineral water	['mɪnərəl wɔ:tə]	Mineralwasser
fish	[fɪʃ]	Fisch
other	['ʌðə]	andere/r/s
summer	['sʌmə]	Sommer
winter	['wɪntə]	Winter

4

to **watch TV**	[ˌwɒtʃ ti:'vi:]	fernsehen
newspaper	['nju:zpeɪpə]	Zeitung
to **play**	[pleɪ]	spielen
to **go**	[gəʊ]	gehen
shower	['ʃaʊə]	Dusche
to **have a shower**	[ˌhəv ə 'ʃaʊə]	duschen
to **phone sb**	[fəʊn]	jdn anrufen
to **use**	[ju:z]	benutzen, gebrauchen
to **have a drink**	[ˌhəv ə 'drɪŋk]	etw trinken

5

morning	['mɔ:nɪŋ]	Morgen
evening	['i:vnɪŋ]	Abend

6

to **speak**	[spi:k]	sprechen
language	['læŋgwɪdʒ]	Sprache
to **work**	[wɜ:k]	arbeiten
hour	['aʊə]	Stunde

7

boy	[bɔɪ]	Junge
girl	[gɜ:l]	Mädchen
game	[geɪm]	Spiel
to **send**	[send]	senden, schicken

Unit 03, Part B

to **drive**	[draɪv]	fahren

1

to **cook**	[kʊk]	kochen, zubereiten
meal	[mi:l]	Mahlzeit, Gericht
piano	[pi'ænəʊ]	Klavier
to **run**	[rʌn]	laufen
marathon	['mærəθən]	Marathon

2

to **agree**	[ə'gri:]	zustimmen
to **disagree**	[ˌdɪsə'gri:]	nicht zustimmen, anderer Meinung sein
possible	['pɒsəbl]	möglich
impossible	[ɪm'pɒsəbl]	unmöglich

3

a little	[ə 'lɪtl]	ein wenig

4

to **count**	[kaʊnt]	zählen
to **name**	[neɪm]	nennen
to **remember sth**	[rɪ'membə]	sich an etw erinnern
last	[lɑ:st]	letzte/r/s

5

to **live**	[lɪv]	leben, wohnen

7

flat	[flæt]	Wohnung

8

diary	['daɪəri]	Terminkalender
to **put sth together**	[ˌpʊt tə'geðə]	etw zusammensetzen
Monday	['mʌndeɪ]	Montag
Tuesday	['tju:zdeɪ]	Dienstag
Wednesday	['wenzdeɪ]	Mittwoch
Thursday	['θɜ:zdeɪ]	Donnerstag
Friday	['fraɪdeɪ]	Freitag
Saturday	['sætədeɪ]	Samstag, Sonnabend
Sunday	['sʌndeɪ]	Sonntag
to **relax**	[rɪ'læks]	sich ausruhen

9

to **swim**	[swɪm]	schwimmen

9 **1.16**

but	[bʌt]	aber, sondern
really	['ri:əli]	wirklich
a lot	[ə 'lɒt]	viel, eine Menge
to **drink**	[drɪŋk]	trinken
great	[greɪt]	großartig, toll

Unit 03, Part C

4

child, children	[tʃaɪld, 'tʃɪldrən]	Kind, Kinder
European	[ˌjʊərə'piːən]	europäisch
Bristol	['brɪstl]	*Stadt in Südwestengland*

6

pie chart	['paɪ tʃɑːt]	Tortendiagramm
to **decide**	[dɪ'saɪd]	entscheiden
to **sleep**	[sliːp]	schlafen
to **eat**	[iːt]	essen
to **be home**	[bɪ 'həʊm]	zu Hause sein
boss	[bɒs]	Chef/in
a couple of	[ə 'kʌpl əv]	ein paar
team	[tiːm]	Mannschaft
all	[ɔːl]	alles
to **love**	[lʌv]	lieben, etw sehr gern mögen

7

survey	['sɜːveɪ]	Umfrage
survey form	['sɜːveɪ fɔːm]	Umfrageformular

7 1.17

Venice	['venɪs]	Venedig

Unit 04, Part A

1

delicious	[dɪ'lɪʃəs]	köstlich, lecker
chips	[tʃɪps]	Pommes frites
rice	[raɪs]	Reis
omelette	['ɒmlət]	Omelette
salad	['sæləd]	Salat
chicken	['tʃɪkɪn]	Huhn, Hühnchen
comment	['kɒment]	Kommentar
lovely	['lʌvli]	wunderbar, herrlich
horrible	['hɒrəbl]	schrecklich

2

ready	['redi]	bereit
to **order**	['ɔːdə]	bestellen
dish	[dɪʃ]	Gericht
waiter	['weɪtə]	Kellner
vegetables	['vedʒtəblz]	Gemüse
sauce	[sɔːs]	Soße
hot	[hɒt]	scharf
to **look**	[lʊk]	aussehen
shop assistant	['ʃɒp əsɪstənt]	Verkäufer/in
meat	[miːt]	Fleisch
waitress	['weɪtrɪs]	Kellnerin
onion	['ʌnjən]	Zwiebel
mushroom	['mʌʃrʊm]	Pilz
just	[dʒʌst]	nur, bloß
vegetarian	[ˌvedʒə'teəriən]	Vegetarier/in
orange	['ɒrɪndʒ]	Apfelsine
banana	[bə'nɑːnə]	Banane
to **want**	[wɒnt]	wollen
mayonnaise	[ˌmeɪə'neɪz]	Mayonnaise
salt	[sɔːlt]	Salz
pepper	['pepə]	Pfeffer
please	[pliːz]	bitte
cheese	[tʃiːz]	Käse
to **mean**	[miːn]	bedeuten, heißen
mustard	['mʌstəd]	Senf

3

to **come**	[kʌm]	kommen

4

carrot	['kærət]	Karotte
potato	[pə'teɪtəʊ]	Kartoffel
strawberry	['strɔːbəri]	Erdbeere
grape	[greɪp]	Traube
tomato	[tə'mɑːtəʊ]	Tomate
bean	[biːn]	Bohne
beef	[biːf]	Rindfleisch
lamb	[læm]	Lamm
pork	[pɔːk]	Schweinefleisch
milk	[mɪlk]	Milch
category	['kætəgəri]	Kategorie

5 1.18

menu	['menjuː]	Speisekarte
thank you	['θæŋk ju]	danke
sir	[sɜː]	mein Herr *(Anrede)*
sure	[ʃʊə]	sicher

Unit 04, Part B

1

shoe	[ʃuː]	Schuh
post office	['pəʊst ɒfɪs]	Postamt
clothes	[kləʊðz]	Kleidung, Kleider
supermarket	['suːpəmɑːkɪt]	Supermarkt
travel agent	['trævl eɪdʒənt]	Reisebüro

2

holidays	['hɒlədeɪz]	Urlaub, Ferien

2 1.19

to **shop for sth**	['ʃɒp fə]	etw kaufen, etw einkaufen (gehen)
wife	[waɪf]	(Ehe-)Frau
to **hate**	[heɪt]	hassen, überhaupt nicht mögen
shop	[ʃɒp]	Laden, Geschäft
well	[wel]	nun, also
why	[waɪ]	warum

4

stamp	[stæmp]	Briefmarke
aspirin	['æsprɪn]	Aspirin
sausage	['sɒsɪdʒ]	Würstchen
bread	[bred]	Brot
chemist	['kemɪst]	Apotheke
butcher	['bʊtʃə]	Metzger
baker	['beɪkə]	Bäcker
newsagent	['njuːzeɪdʒənt]	Zeitungshändler
almost	['ɔːlməʊst]	fast, beinahe
everything	['evriθɪŋ]	alles
bank	[bæŋk]	Bank
near	[nɪə]	in der Nähe, nahe
lots of	['lɒts əv]	viele
there is/are	[ðeər 'ɪz/'ɑː]	es gibt

5

lift	[lɪft]	Aufzug
upstairs	[ˌʌp'steəz]	oben

6

to **buy**	[baɪ]	kaufen
postcard	['pəʊstkɑːd]	Postkarte
to **change**	[tʃeɪndʒ]	wechseln
money	['mʌni]	Geld
petrol	['petrəl]	Benzin
area	['eəriə]	Gegend, Gebiet

7

to **cost**	[kɒst]	kosten
to **pay**	[peɪ]	zahlen, bezahlen
much	[mʌtʃ]	viel
to **look**	[lʊk]	sich umschauen
credit card	['kredɪt kɑːd]	Kreditkarte

Unit word list

of course	[əf 'kɔ:s]	natürlich, selbstverständlich
problem	['prɒbləm]	Problem
no	[nəʊ]	kein
You're welcome.	[jɔ: 'welkəm]	Bitte.

8

park	[pɑ:k]	Park

Unit 04, Part C

1

a lot	[ə 'lɒt]	*hier:* häufig
India	['ɪndiə]	Indien

2

customer	['kʌstəmə]	Kunde/Kundin, Gast

3

type	[taɪp]	Art, Sorte

4

pea	[pi:]	Erbse
lettuce	['letɪs]	Kopfsalat

5

juice	[dʒu:s]	Saft

5 1.20

to **think**	[θɪŋk]	denken, glauben
idea	[aɪ'dɪə]	Idee
to **let**	[let]	lassen
let's … (let us …)	[lets]	lass uns/lassen Sie uns …
some	[sʌm]	etwas, einige
certainly	['sɜ:tnli]	sicher(-lich), gewiss

Unit 05, Part A

1

bedroom	['bedru:m]	Schlafzimmer
bathroom	['bɑ:θru:m]	Badezimmer
kitchen	['kɪtʃɪn]	Küche
hall	[hɔ:l]	Diele, Flur
living room	['lɪvɪŋ ru:m]	Wohnzimmer
winter garden	['wɪntə gɑ:dn]	Wintergarten

2

home	[həʊm]	Heim, Zuhause, Haus, Wohnung
modern	['mɒdn]	modern
son	[sʌn]	Sohn
washing machine	['wɒʃɪŋ məʃi:n]	Waschmaschine
fridge	[frɪdʒ]	Kühlschrank
cooker	['kʊkə]	Herd
table	['teɪbl]	Tisch
sofa	['səʊfə]	Sofa
sofa-bed	['səʊfə bed]	Schlafsofa
so	[səʊ]	sodass
bath	[bɑ:θ]	Badewanne
to **have got**	[həv gɒt]	haben, (etw) besitzen
big	[bɪg]	groß
balcony	['bælkəni]	Balkon
because	[bɪ'kɒz]	weil, da

5

gym	[dʒɪm]	Fitnessklub
toilet	['tɔɪlət]	Toilette

5 1.21

What about …?	['wɒt əbaʊt]	Was ist mit …?
easy	['i:zi]	leicht
bed	[bed]	Bett
centre	['sentə]	Mitte, Zentrum
swimming pool	['swɪmɪŋ pu:l]	Schwimmbad

Unit 05, Part B

1

husband	['hʌzbənd]	(Ehe-)Mann
mother	['mʌðə]	Mutter
daughter	['dɔ:tə]	Tochter
the same	[ðə 'seɪm]	der/die/dasselbe
hair	[heə]	Haar(e)
sister	['sɪstə]	Schwester
our	['aʊə]	unser/e/s
dog	[dɒg]	Hund
brother	['brʌðə]	Bruder
photo	['fəʊtəʊ]	Foto
university	[ˌju:nɪ'vɜ:səti]	Universität

3

grandchild, grandchildren	['græntʃaɪld, 'græntʃɪldrən]	Enkel/in, Enkel
father	['fɑ:ðə]	Vater
to **test**	[test]	prüfen, testen

4

animal	['ænɪml]	Tier
cat	[kæt]	Katze
grandparent	['grænpeərənt]	Großvater/-mutter
parents	['peərənts]	Eltern

5 1.22

old	[əʊld]	alt
young	[jʌŋ]	jung
happy	['hæpi]	zufrieden, froh, glücklich
long	[lɒŋ]	lang
boyfriend	['bɔɪfrend]	Freund

6

bag	[bæg]	Tasche
briefcase	['bri:fkeɪs]	Aktentasche

7

customs	['kʌstəmz]	Zoll
mirror	['mɪrə]	Spiegel
key	[ki:]	Schlüssel
perfume	['pɜ:fju:m]	Parfüm
hairbrush	['heəbrʌʃ]	Haarbürste
glasses	['glɑ:sɪz]	Brille
bus	[bʌs]	Bus
ticket	['tɪkɪt]	Fahrkarte
purse	[pɜ:s]	Portmonee, Geldbeutel *(für Damen)*
wallet	['wɒlɪt]	Portmonee, Geldbeutel *(für Herren)*
lipstick	['lɪpstɪk]	Lippenstift
umbrella	[ʌm'brelə]	Regenschirm

10

rucksack	['rʌksæk]	Rucksack

Unit 05, Part C

4

passport	['pɑ:spɔ:t]	Reisepass

6

greeting	['gri:tɪŋ]	Gruß
wonderful	['wʌndəfl]	wunderbar
special	['speʃl]	besondere/r/s

to **hope**	[həʊp]	hoffen
year	[jɪə]	Jahr
good luck	[ˌgʊd 'lʌk]	viel Glück
exam	[ɪg'zæm]	Prüfung
congratulations	[kənˌgrætʃu'leɪʃnz]	herzlichen Glückwunsch

7

grandparents	['grænpeərənts]	Großeltern

8

doctor	['dɒktə]	Arzt/Ärztin
best	[best]	beste/r/s

Unit 06, Part A

public	['pʌblɪk]	öffentlich
private	['praɪvət]	privat
transport	['trænspɔ:t]	Verkehr, Verkehrsmittel, Beförderungsmittel

1

ship	[ʃɪp]	Schiff
bike	[baɪk]	Fahrrad
foot	[fʊt]	Fuß
underground	['ʌndəgraʊnd]	U-Bahn
train	[treɪn]	Zug
tram	[træm]	Straßenbahn
to **put**	[pʊt]	setzen, stellen
means of transport	[ˌmi:nz əf 'trænspɔ:t]	Verkehrsmittel
slow	[sləʊ]	langsam
fast	[fɑ:st]	schnell
cheap	[tʃi:p]	billig, preiswert
expensive	[ɪk'spensɪv]	teuer

2

green	[gri:n]	grün
to **go**	[gəʊ]	gehen, reisen
small	[smɔ:l]	klein
to **walk**	[wɔ:k]	zu Fuß gehen, laufen

3

to **need**	[ni:d]	benötigen, brauchen
Scotland	['skɒtlənd]	Schottland
to **get home**	[get 'həʊm]	nach Hause gelangen
public transport	[ˌpʌblɪk 'trænspɔ:t]	öffentlicher Personennahverkehr

4

always	['ɔ:lweɪz]	immer, stets
to **go on holiday**	[ˌgəʊ ɒn 'hɒlədeɪ]	in den Urlaub fahren
never	['nevə]	nie
to **fly**	[flaɪ]	fliegen
normally	['nɔ:məli]	normalerweise
sometimes	['sʌmtaɪmz]	manchmal
to **take**	[teɪk]	nehmen
statement	['steɪtmənt]	Aussage
on foot	[ɒn 'fʊt]	zu Fuß
after	['ɑ:ftə]	nach
work	[wɜ:k]	Arbeit

5

everywhere	['evriweə]	überallhin
most	[məʊst]	die meisten
every	['evri]	jede/r/s
to **sail**	[seɪl]	mit dem Schiff fahren
to **cycle**	['saɪkl]	radfahren

6 1.23

tomorrow	[tə'mɒrəʊ]	morgen
start	[stɑ:t]	Beginn, Anfang
Lucky you.	[ˌlʌki 'ju:]	Du Glückliche/r.
plan	[plæn]	Plan
to **leave**	[li:v]	abfahren, abfliegen
first	[fɜ:st]	zuerst
station	['steɪʃn]	Bahnhof
to **take**	[teɪk]	dauern
That's it.	[ˌðæts 'ɪt]	Das war's./Das ist alles.
to **get**	[get]	bekommen, besorgen
south	[saʊθ]	Süden
Sicily	['sɪsəli]	Sizilien

7

to **go**	[gəʊ]	führen
line	[laɪn]	Linie
blue	[blu:]	blau
yellow	['jeləʊ]	gelb
stop	[stɒp]	Haltestelle
there	[ðeə]	dort, dorthin

8

How much is/are …?	[haʊ 'mʌtʃ ɪz/ɑ:]	Wie viel kostet/kosten …?
to **travel**	['trævl]	reisen, fahren
first	[fɜ:st]	erste/r/s
class	[klɑ:s]	Klasse
Sorry.	['sɒri]	Tut mir leid.
about	[ə'baʊt]	ungefähr

Unit 06, Part B

1

month	[mʌnθ]	Monat
season	['si:zn]	Jahreszeit
autumn	['ɔ:təm]	Herbst
January	['dʒænjuəri]	Januar
February	['februəri]	Februar
March	[mɑ:tʃ]	März
April	['eɪprəl]	April
May	[meɪ]	Mai
June	[dʒu:n]	Juni
July	[dʒu'laɪ]	Juli
August	['ɔ:gəst]	August
September	[sep'tembə]	September
October	[ɒk'təʊbə]	Oktober
November	[nəʊ'vembə]	November
December	[dɪ'sembə]	Dezember
spring	[sprɪŋ]	Frühling

2

new	[nju:]	neu
New Year	[nju: 'jɪə]	Neujahr
to **start**	[stɑ:t]	beginnen
Christmas	['krɪsməs]	Weihnachten
birthday	['bɜ:θdeɪ]	Geburtstag
skiing	['ski:ɪŋ]	Skifahren

3

tree	[tri:]	Baum
gold	[gəʊld]	gold(en)
to **rain**	[reɪn]	regnen
cold	[kəʊld]	kalt
very	['veri]	sehr
hot	[hɒt]	heiß
sunny	['sʌni]	sonnig
to **snow**	[snəʊ]	schneien
Egypt	['i:dʒɪpt]	Ägypten
Sweden	['swi:dn]	Schweden
New England	[ˌnju: 'ɪŋglənd]	Neuengland
weather	['weðə]	Wetter

5

beach	[bi:tʃ]	Strand
city break	['sɪti breɪk]	Städteurlaub
guide book	['gaɪd bʊk]	Reiseführer
skis	[ski:z]	Skier

Unit word list

hat	[hæt]	Mütze, Hut
glove	[glʌv]	Handschuh
scarf	[skɑ:f]	Schal
warm	[wɔ:m]	warm
sleeping bag	['sli:pɪŋ bæg]	Schlafsack
torch	[tɔ:tʃ]	Taschenlampe
tent	[tent]	Zelt
towel	['taʊəl]	Handtuch
sunglasses	['sʌnglɑ:sɪz]	Sonnenbrille
culture	['kʌltʃə]	Kultur
sun	[sʌn]	Sonne
nothing	['nʌθɪŋ]	nichts
sea	[si:]	Meer
to **feel**	[fi:l]	(sich) fühlen
I feel hot.	[aɪ ˌfi:l 'hɒt]	Mir ist warm.
Austria	['ɒstriə]	Österreich
snow	[snəʊ]	Schnee
busy	['bɪzi]	belebt, hektisch
noise	[nɔɪz]	Lärm
simple	['sɪmpl]	einfach
perfect	['pɜ:fɪkt]	perfekt

6 **1.25**

to **prefer**	[prɪ'fɜ:]	vorziehen, lieber mögen
week	[wi:k]	Woche
mountain	['maʊntən]	Berg
Greece	[gri:s]	Griechenland
Turkey	['tɜ:ki]	Türkei

7

to **take sth**	[teɪk]	etw mitnehmen

Countries, places and nationalities

Africa	['æfrɪkə]	Afrika
America	[ə'merɪkə]	Amerika
American	[ə'merɪkən]	amerikanisch
Argentina	[ˌɑːdʒən'tiːnə]	Argentinien
Asia	['eɪʃə]	Asien
Asian	['eɪʃn]	asiatisch
Australasia	[ˌɒstrə'leɪʃə]	Australien, Neuseeland und Ozeanien
Australia	[ɒ'streɪliə]	Australien
Austria	['ɒstriə]	Österreich
Birmingham	['bɜːmɪŋəm]	Stadt in Mittelengland
Brazil	[brə'zɪl]	Brasilien
Bristol	['brɪstl]	Stadt in Südwestengland
British	['brɪtɪʃ]	britisch
Bulgaria	[bʌl'geəriə]	Bulgarien
Bulgarian	[bʌl'geəriən]	bulgarisch
Canada	['kænədə]	Kanada
China	['tʃaɪnə]	China
Chinese	[tʃaɪ'niːz]	chinesisch, Chinese, Chinesin
the Coliseum	[ˌkɒlə'siəm]	das Kolosseum (in Rom)
Colombia	[kə'lɒmbiə]	Kolumbien
Croatia	[krəʊ'eɪʃə]	Kroatien
Croatian	[krəʊ'eɪʃən]	kroatisch
Edinburgh	['edɪnbərə]	Hauptstadt Schottlands
Egypt	['iːdʒɪpt]	Ägypten
England	['ɪŋglənd]	England
English	['ɪŋglɪʃ]	englisch
Europe	['jʊərəp]	Europa
European	[ˌjʊərə'piːən]	europäisch
France	[frɑːns]	Frankreich
French	[frentʃ]	französisch
German	['dʒɜːmən]	deutsch
Germany	['dʒɜːməni]	Deutschland
Glasgow	['glɑːsgəʊ]	größte Stadt Schottlands
Greece	[griːs]	Griechenland
India	['ɪndiə]	Indien
Italian	[ɪ'tæljən]	italienisch
Italy	['ɪtəli]	Italien
Japan	[dʒə'pæn]	Japan
Japanese	[ˌdʒæpə'niːz]	japanisch
Lisbon	['lɪzbən]	Lissabon
Liverpool	['lɪvəpuːl]	Stadt in Nordwestengland
Manchester	['mæntʃɪstə]	Stadt in Nordwestengland
Milan	[mɪ'læn]	Mailand
Mongolia	[mɒŋ'gəʊliə]	Mongolei
Morocco	[mə'rɒkəʊ]	Marokko
Moscow	['mɒskəʊ]	Moskau
Munich	['mjuːnɪk]	München
New England	[ˌnjuː 'ɪŋglənd]	Neuengland
New Zealand	[ˌnjuː 'ziːlənd]	Neuseeland
North America	[ˌnɔːθ ə'merɪkə]	Nordamerika
Poland	['pəʊlənd]	Polen
Polish	['pəʊlɪʃ]	polnisch
Rome	[rəʊm]	Rom
Scotland	['skɒtlənd]	Schottland
Sicily	['sɪsəli]	Sizilien
South Africa	[ˌsaʊθ 'æfrɪkə]	Südafrika
South America	[ˌsaʊθ ə'merɪkə]	Südamerika
South American	[ˌsaʊθ ə'merɪkən]	südamerikanisch
Spain	[speɪn]	Spanien
Spanish	['spænɪʃ]	spanisch
Sweden	['swiːdn]	Schweden
Swiss	[swɪs]	schweizerisch
Switzerland	['swɪtsələnd]	Schweiz
Tunisia	[tju'nɪziə]	Tunesien
Turkey	['tɜːki]	Türkei
the United States	[ðə juˌnaɪtɪd 'steɪts]	die Vereinigten Staaten
Venice	['venɪs]	Venedig
Vienna	[vi'enə]	Wien

A Alphabetical word list

A

about über, ungefähr 1A
What about …? Was ist mit …? 5A
across (Kreuzworträtsel) quer 1C
activity Tätigkeit, Aktivität 3A
to add hinzufügen 3A
address Adresse 2A
after nach 6A
afternoon Nachmittag 1B
again wieder 2B
to agree zustimmen 3B
airport Flughafen 2C
all alles 3C
almost fast, beinahe 4B
always immer, stets 6A
am bin 1A
and und 1A
animal Tier 5B
another andere/r/s 1B
answer Antwort 1B
to answer antworten 1B
apple Apfel 1A
April April 6B
are bist, sind, seid 1A
area Gegend, Gebiet 4B
to ask fragen 1B
aspirin Aspirin 4B
at home zu Hause 5A
August August 6B
autumn Herbst 6B

B

bag Tasche 5B
baker Bäcker/in 4B
balcony Balkon 5A
banana Banane 4A
bank Bank 4B
bath Badewanne 5A
bathroom Badezimmer 5A
beach Strand 6B
bean Bohne 4A
because weil, da 5A
bed Bett 5A
bedroom Schlafzimmer 5A
beef Rindfleisch 4A
beer Bier 1A
to belong to sb jdm gehören 5B
best beste/r/s 5C
big groß 5A
bike Fahrrad 6A
birthday Geburtstag 6B
blue blau 6A
boarding card Bordkarte 2C
book Buch 1A
born geboren 2B
boss Chef/in 3C
boy Junge 3A
boyfriend Freund 5B
bread Brot 4B
bridge Brücke 2C
briefcase Aktentasche 5B
brother Bruder 5B
bus Bus 5B
busy belebt, hektisch 6B
but aber, sondern 3B
butcher Metzger/in 4B
to buy kaufen 4B
bye tschüs 1A

C

café Café 2C
to call out (laut) sagen 1B
can können 1A
capital Hauptstadt 2C
car Auto 1A
car hire Autovermietung 1B
car park Parkplatz, Parkhaus, Tiefgarage 2C
card Karte 1C
carefully aufmerksam 2A
carrot Karotte 4A
cat Katze 5B
category Kategorie 4A
cathedral Dom, Kathedrale 2A
centre Mitte, Zentrum 5A
certainly sicher(-lich), gewiss 4C
chair Stuhl 1A
to change ändern, wechseln 3A
chart Übersicht 1B
cheap billig, preiswert 6A
cheese Käse 4A
chemist Apotheke 4B
chewing gum Kaugummi 5B
chicken Huhn, Hühnchen 4A
child, children Kind, Kinder 3C
chips Pommes frites 4A
chocolate Schokolade, Praline 1A
to choose wählen 2B
Christmas Weihnachten 6B
cinema Kino 2A
city Stadt 1B
city break Städteurlaub 6B
city tour Stadtrundfahrt 2B
class Kurs, Klasse 1A
classical klassisch 3A
classmate Klassenkamerad/in 1A
clothes Kleidung, Kleider 4B
coffee Kaffee 1A
cold kalt 6B
coloured farbig 3C
column Spalte 3A
to come kommen 4A
comment Kommentar 4A
to complete vervollständigen, ausfüllen 1B
congratulations (herzlichen) Glückwunsch 5C
continent Kontinent 1C
conversation Unterhaltung, Gespräch 3B
to cook kochen, zubereiten 3B
cooker Herd 5A
copy Exemplar, Kopie 1B
correct richtig, korrekt 4B
to correct korrigieren 2C
to cost kosten 4B
to count zählen 2A
country Land 1B
couple, a ~ of ein paar 3C
course, of ~ natürlich, selbstverständlich 4B
credit card Kreditkarte 4B
to cross ankreuzen 5C
culture Kultur 6B
customer Kunde/Kundin 4C
customs Zoll 5B
to cycle radfahren 6A

D

daughter Tochter 5B
day Tag 3A
December Dezember 6B
to decide entscheiden 3C
delicious köstlich, lecker 4A
description Beschreibung 4C
desk Pult, Schreibtisch 5B
destination Zielort 2C
dialogue Dialog 1A
diary Terminkalender 3B
different andere/r/s, unterschiedliche/r/s 2B
to disagree nicht zustimmen, anderer Meinung sein 3B
dish Gericht 4A
doctor Arzt/Ärztin 5C
dog Hund 5B
down (Kreuzworträtsel) senkrecht 1C
downstairs unten 5C
drink Getränk 3A
to have a ~ etw trinken 3A
to drink trinken 3B
to drive fahren 3B

E

each jede/r/s 2A
each time jeweils 1C
Easter Ostern 6B
easy leicht 5A
to eat essen 3C
evening Abend 3A
every jede/r/s 6A
everyone jede/r/s 2B
everything alles 4B
everywhere überall 6A
exam Prüfung 5C
to excuse entschuldigen 2B
Excuse me. Entschuldigung./ Verzeihung. 2B
expensive teuer 6A

F

false falsch 2B
family Familie 1B
famous berühmt 2B
fantastic fantastisch 2B
fast schnell 6A
father Vater 5B
favourite Lieblings- 1B
February Februar 6B
to feel (sich) fühlen 6B
I ~ hot. Mir ist warm. 6B
female weiblich 1C
finally schließlich, zu guter Letzt 1A
to find finden 1C
to find out herausfinden 6B
first zuerst, erste/r/s 6A
first name Vorname 1B
fish Fisch 3A
flat Wohnung 3B
flight Flug 2C
to fly fliegen 6A
following folgende/r/s 1B
food Essen 3A
foot Fuß 6A
on foot zu Fuß 6A
football Fußball 3A
for für 1B
form Form, Formular 1B
Friday Freitag 3B
fridge Kühlschrank 5A
friend Freund/in 2B
from von, aus 1B
fruit Obst, Frucht, Früchte 1A

G

game Spiel 3A
gap Lücke 2C
garden Garten 1A
gate Tor, hier: Flugsteig 2C
Genghis Khan Dschingis Khan 1C
to get bekommen, besorgen 6A
to get home nach Hause gelangen 6A
girl Mädchen 3A
glasses Brille 5B
glove Handschuh 6B
to go gehen, reisen, führen 3A
to go on holiday in den Urlaub fahren 6A
gold gold(en) 6B
good gut 1A
good luck viel Glück 5C
Goodbye. Auf Wiedersehen. 1A
grandchild, grandchildren Enkel/in, Enkel 5B
grandparent Großvater/ -mutter 5B
grandparents Großeltern 5C
grape Traube 4A
great großartig, toll 3B
green grün 6A
greeting Gruß 5C
grid Gitter 4B
group Gruppe 6B
guide Reiseführer/in 2B
guide book Reiseführer 6B
gym Fitnessklub 5A

H

hair Haar(e) 5B
hairbrush Haarbürste 5B
half, halves Hälfte, Hälften 6B
hall Diele, Flur 5A
happy zufrieden, froh, glücklich 5B
hat Mütze, Hut 6B
to hate hassen, überhaupt nicht mögen 4B
to have haben 1B
to have got haben, (etw) besitzen 5A
to have sth with you etw bei sich haben 1B
to have a drink etw trinken 3A
to have a shower duschen 3A
to hear hören 1B
hello hallo 1A
to say ~ to sb jdn begrüßen 1A
to help helfen 1B
here hier 1B
Here you are. Bitte sehr. 1B
to highlight hervorheben, markieren 3A
holiday, to go on ~ in den Urlaub fahren 6A
holidays Urlaub, Ferien 4B
home Heim, Zuhause, Haus, Wohnung 5A
to be ~ zu Hause sein 3C
to get ~ nach Hause gelangen 6A
to hope hoffen 5C
horrible schrecklich 4A
hot scharf, heiß 4A
I feel ~. Mir ist warm. 6B
hotel Hotel 2A
hour Stunde 3A
house Haus 1A
how wie 1A
How are you? Wie geht es dir/euch/Ihnen? 1A

How much is/are …? 6A
Wie viel kostet/kosten …?
husband (Ehe-)Mann 5B

I

I ich 1A
I'm ich bin 1A
idea Idee 4C
impossible unmöglich 3B
information Angaben 2A
interest Interesse 3A
interesting interessant 2B
to introduce sb jdn vorstellen 2B
is ist 1A
it es 2A

J

January Januar 6B
juice Saft 4C
July Juli 6B
June Juni 6B
just nur, bloß 4A

K

to keep behalten 1B
key Schlüssel 5B
kitchen Küche 5A
to know wissen, kennen 2B

L

lamb Lamm 4A
language Sprache 3A
last letzte/r/s 3B
to leave abfahren, abfliegen 6A
lesson (Unterrichts-)Stunde 1B
to let lassen 4C
let's … (let us …) lass uns/lassen Sie uns … 4C
letter Buchstabe 1B
lettuce Kopfsalat 4C
lift Aufzug 4B
to like sth etw mögen 3A
line Zeile, Linie 2C
lipstick Lippenstift 5B
to listen zuhören 1A
little klein 1C
a ~ ein wenig 3B
to live leben, wohnen 3B
living room Wohnzimmer 5A
logical logisch 5C
long lang 5B
to look aussehen, sich umschauen 4A
to look at sth sich etw ansehen 2A
lot, a ~ viel, eine Menge, sehr, häufig 3B
lots of viele 4B
lounge Wartesaal, -halle 2C
to love lieben, sehr gern mögen 3C
lovely wunderbar, herrlich 4A
luck, good ~ viel Glück 5C
Lucky you. Du Glückliche/r. 6A

M

to make machen, bilden 1A
many viele 1A
map Plan, Karte 4B
marathon Marathon 3B
March März 6B
market Markt 2A
May Mai 6B
to match zuordnen 1A
mayonnaise Mayonnaise 4A
me ich, mich 5B
meal Mahlzeit, Gericht 3B
to mean bedeuten, heißen 4A
meaning Bedeutung 6A
means of transport Verkehrsmittel 6A
meat Fleisch 4A
to meet sb jdm begegnen 1A
Nice to meet you. Schön, dich/Sie kennen zu lernen. 1A
menu Speisekarte 4A
mermaid Meerjungfrau 1C
milk Milch 4A
mineral water Mineralwasser 3A
minute Minute 2B
mirror Spiegel 5B
missing fehlend 2B
to be ~ fehlen 2B
mistake Fehler 2C
mobile Handy, Mobiltelefon 2A
modern modern 5A
Monday Montag 3B
money Geld 4B
month Monat 6B
morning Morgen 3A
most die meisten 6A
mother Mutter 5B
mountain Berg 6B
Mr Herr 1B
Ms Frau 1B
much viel 4B
museum Museum 2A
mushroom Pilz 4A
music Musik 1A
mustard Senf 4A
my mein

N

name Name 1A
first ~ Vorname 1B
to name nennen 3B
nationality Staatsangehörigkeit 1B
near in der Nähe, nahe 4B
to need benötigen, brauchen 6A
never nie 6A
new neu 6B
newsagent Zeitungshändler/in 4B
newspaper Zeitung 3A
nice nett, hübsch, schön 1A
Nice to meet you. Schön, dich/Sie kennen zu lernen. 1A
no nein, kein 1B
noise Lärm 6B
normally normalerweise 6A
not nicht 1A
nothing nichts 6B
November November 6B
now jetzt 2B
number Nummer, Zahl 2A
~ plate Nummernschild 2A
to number nummerieren 1A

O

object Gegenstand 1A
October Oktober 6B
of course natürlich, selbstverständlich 4B
office Büro 1B
old alt 5B
omelette Omelette 4A
one eine/r/s, eins 1B
onion Zwiebel 4A
opera Oper 2A
opera house Opernhaus 2C
or oder 1A
orange Apfelsine 4A
order Reihenfolge 4A
to order bestellen 4A
other andere/r/s 3A
our unser/e/s 5B

P

pair Paar 5B
in ~s paarweise 5B
parents Eltern 5B
park Park 4B
passport Reisepass 5C
to pay zahlen, bezahlen 4B
pea Erbse 4C
pen Stift 1A
people Personen, Leute 4C
pepper Pfeffer 4A
perfect perfekt 6B
perfume Parfüm 5B
person Person 4B
petrol Benzin 4B
to phone sb jdn anrufen 3A
phone number Telefonnummer 2A
photo Foto 5B
piano Klavier 3B
picture Bild 1A
pie chart Tortendiagramm 3C
place Ort, Platz, Zuhause 1A
plan Plan 6A
plane Flugzeug 2C
to play spielen 3A
please bitte 4A
pork Schweinefleisch 4A
possible möglich 3B
post office Postamt 4B
postcard Postkarte 4B
potato Kartoffel 4A
to practise üben 1A
to prefer vorziehen, lieber mögen 6B
private privat 6A
problem Problem 4B
pub Kneipe 2A
public öffentlich 6A
public transport öffentlicher Personennahverkehr 6A
purse Portemonnaie, Geldbeutel (für Damen) 5B
to put setzen, stellen 6A
to put sth together etw zusammensetzen 3B

Q

question Frage 1B

R

to rain regnen 6B
to read lesen 1A
to read sth out etw vorlesen 2A
ready bereit 4A
real wirklich, wahr, richtig 2B
really wirklich 3B
records Unterlagen 1B
red rot 2C
to relax sich ausruhen 3B
to remember sth sich an etw erinnern 3B
to repeat wiederholen, nachsprechen 1A
restaurant Restaurant 2A
rice Reis 4A
right richtig 2B
room Zimmer, Raum 5A
rucksack Rucksack 5B
to run laufen 3B

S

to sail mit dem Schiff fahren 6A
salad Salat 4A
salt Salz 4A
same, the ~ der/die/dasselbe 5B
Saturday Samstag, Sonnabend 3B
sauce Soße 4A
sausage Würstchen 4B
to say sagen 1A
to say hello to sb jdn begrüßen 1A
scarf Schal 6B
school Schule 2A
sea Meer 6B
season Jahreszeit 6B
seat Sitz, Platz 2C
to see hier: verstehen 2C
to send senden, schicke 3A
sentence Satz 1A
September September 6B
sequence Reihenfolge 6A
ship Schiff 6A
shoe Schuh 4B
shop Laden, Geschäft 4B
shop assistant Verkäufer/in 4A
to shop for sth etw kaufen, etw einkaufen (gehen) 4B
shopping Einkaufen 2B
shopping list Einkaufszettel 1A
shopping centre Einkaufszentrum 4B
short kurz 2A
to show zeigen 1B
shower Dusche 3A
to have a ~ duschen 3A
simple einfach 6B
sir mein Herr 4A
sister Schwester 5B
skiing Skifahren 6B
skis Skier 6B
to sleep schlafen 3C
sleeping bag Schlafsack 6B
slow langsam 6A
small klein 6A
snow Schnee 6B
to snow schneien 6B
so sodass 5A
sofa Sofa 5A
sofa-bed Schlafsofa 5A
some etwas 4C
sometimes manchmal 6A
son Sohn 5A
Sorry. Tut mir leid. 6A
south Süden 6A
to speak sprechen 3A
speaker Person, die (gerade) spricht 1C
special besondere/r/s 5C
to spell buchstabieren 1B
sports Sport 3A
spring Frühling 6B
square Platz 2C

Alphabetical word list

stamp *Briefmarke* 4B
start *Beginn, Anfang* 6A
to **start** *beginnen* 6B
statement *Aussage* 6A
station *Bahnhof* 6A
stop *Haltestelle* 6A
strawberry *Erdbeere* 4A
street *Straße* 1B
student *Schüler/in, Student/in, Kursteilnehmer/in* 1B
summer *Sommer* 3A
sun *Sonne* 6B
Sunday *Sonntag* 3B
sunglasses *Sonnenbrille* 6B
sunny *sonnig* 6B
supermarket *Supermarkt* 4B
sure *sicher* 4A
survey *Umfrage* 3C
to **swim** *schwimmen* 3B
swimming pool *Schwimmbad* 5A

T

table *Tisch* 5A
to **take** *nehmen, dauern* 6A
to **take sth** *etw mitnehmen* 6B
Take care. *Pass auf dich/ Passen Sie auf sich auf.* 1A
to **talk** *sprechen* 5A
taxi *Taxi* 1A
tea *Tee* 1A
teacher *Leherer/in* 2B
team *Mannschaft* 3C
telephone *Telefon* 2A
to **tell** *erzählen, sagen* 1B
tennis *Tennis* 3A
tent *Zelt* 6B
to **test** *prüfen, testen* 5B
thank you *danke* 4A
thanks *danke* 1A
That's it. *Das war's. Das ist alles.* 6A
the *der, die, das* 1A
theatre *Theater* 2A
then *dann* 1A
there *dort, dorthin* 6A
there is/are *es gibt* 4B
thing *Ding* 1B
to **think** *denken, glauben* 4C
this *dies, diese/r/s* 1A
Thursday *Donnerstag* 3B
to **tick** *mit einem Häkchen versehen* 1A
ticket *Fahrkarte* 5B
time *Zeit* 2B
tissue *Papiertaschentuch* 5B
today *heute* 2B
toilet *Toilette* 5A
tomato *Tomate* 4A
tomorrow *morgen* 6A
…, too *auch, ebenso* 1A
torch *Taschenlampe* 6B
tourist *Tourist/in* 4B
towel *Handtuch* 6B
tower *Turm* 2A
train *Zug* 6A
tram *Straßenbahn* 6A
transport *Verkehr, Verkehrsmittel, Beförderungsmittel* 6A
means of ~ *Verkehrsmittel* 6A
public ~ *öffentlicher Personennahverkehr* 6A
to **travel** *reisen, fahren* 6A
travel agent *Reisebüro* 4B
tree *Baum* 6B
true *richtig, wahr* 2B
Tuesday *Dienstag* 3B
to **turn around** *sich umdrehen* 5B
type *Art, Sorte* 4C

U

umbrella *Regenschirm* 5B
underground *U-Bahn* 6A
underlined *unterstrichen* 5C
university *Universität* 5B
to **unscramble** *entknoten* 1C
upstairs *oben* 4B
to **use** *benutzen, gebrauchen* 3A

V

vegetables *Gemüse* 4A
vegetarian *Vegetarier/in* 4A
very *sehr* 6B
to **visit** *besuchen, besichtigen* 2B

W

waiter *Kellner* 4A
waitress *Kellnerin* 4A
to **walk** *zu Fuß gehen, laufen* 6A
wallet *Portemonnaie, Geldbeutel (für Herren)* 5B
to **want** *wollen* 4A
warm *warm* 6B
was *wurde, war* 2B
washing machine *Waschmaschine* 5A
to **watch TV** *fernsehen* 3A
water *Wasser* 1A
weather *Wetter* 6B
Wednesday *Mittwoch* 3B
week *Woche* 6B
welcome, You're ~ *Bitte.* 4B
well *nun, also* 4B
what *was* 1B
when *wenn* 1B
where *wo* 2B
which *welche/r/s* 1A
white *weiß* 2A
who *wer* 1B
why *warum* 4B
wife *(Ehe-)Frau* 4B
wine *Wein* 1A
winter *Winter* 3A
winter garden *Wintergarten* 5A
with *mit* 1A
wonderful *wunderbar* 5C
word *Wort* 1A
work *Arbeit* 6A
to **work** *arbeiten* 3A
to **write** *schreiben, aufschreiben, notieren* 2A
to **write down** *notieren, aufschreiben* 4C
wrong *falsch* 1C

Y

year *Jahr* 5C
yellow *gelb* 6A
yes *ja* 1B
you *du, ihr, Sie* 1A
you're (you are) *du bist, ihr seid, Sie sind* 1B
young *jung* 5B
your *dein, euer, Ihr* 1B

Bildquellen:

Titelbild:
Corbis/Chris Collins

S. 6 © iStockphoto, Uyen Le, © 123rf, Yury Shirokov, © iStockphoto, © Fotolia, Irina Fischer / Jacques Palut, © adpic, H. Kater, © Fotolia, kmit, © Corbis RF, © Fotolia, © shutterstock, V.J. Matthew, © Fotolia, luchshen, © Alamy, National Geographic Image Collection, © shutterstock, Ewa Walicka; S. 7 © Alamy, National Geographic Image Collection; S. 8 © shutterstock, wavebreakmedia ltd (2); S 9 © shutterstock, ansar80, oliveromg, Mircea Bezergheanu, AISPIX, oliveromg, Warren Goldswain, Rocketclips Inc, Tyler Olson, StockLite; S. 10 © Wikimedia - gemeinfrei, © picture-alliance, Arco Images GmbH, dpa, Arco Images GmbH; S. 11 © Wikimedia – gemeinfrei, © shutterstock, Audi Dela Cruz, titus manea, © Wikimedia; S.12 © shutterstock, sabri denizkizil, Kira-N, Asia Glab, Borat, TeddyandMia, Edyta Pawlowska; S. 13 © shutterstock, Kira-N, Johanna Goodyear; © Fotolia, khz; © iStockphoto, Kevin Klöpper, Joshua Blake, eva serrabassa, © shutterstock, Losevky Pavel, piotrwzk, © iStockphoto, Kevin Klöpper, © shutterstock, Andrei Nekrassov, © iStockphoto, Bruce Bean; S. 14 © Alamy, Coollife; S. 15 © shutterstock, Alberto Zometta, igor kisselev, Felix Mizioznikov, Darren Baker, Marianne Campolongo; S. 16 © iStockphoto, Nikada, © Fotolia, Kheng Guan Toh, Monkey Business, Scanrail, Zoe; S. 17 © iStockphoto, Ramon Berk, © Fotolia, Ewa Walicka; S. 18 © Chetan Kumar; S. 19 © Mark Wolters; S. 20 © iStockphoto, Paul Gregg, © shutterstock, Arkady, Poleze, AISPIX, terekhov igor, Dmitriy Shironosov, Tito Wong; S. 21 © iStockphoto, Paul Gregg, © shutterstock, Yuri Arcurs, IKO, Dmitriy Shironosov, Deklofenak; S. 22 © Fotolia, danielschoenen, © shutterstock, Kuzma; S. 23 © adpic, K. Brümmer, © Fotolia, Ilan Amith, © shutterstock, GMEVIPHOTO, Pakhnyushcha, © iStockphoto, sumnersgraphicsinc; S. 24 © shutterstock, Monkey Business Images, Konstantin Sutyagin; S. 25 © shutterstock, Andresr, oliveromg; S. 26 © shutterstock, Nayashkova Olga, © iStockphoto, Olga Nayashkova, © shutterstock, Alaettin YILDIRIM, Joe Gough, Nikola Bilic, © Fotolia, msheldrake, © shutterstock, PHB.cz (Richard Semik), © Fotofinder, Scholz/ teamwork, © iStockphoto, Steve Debenport; S. 27 © shutterstock, Robyn Mackenzie; S. 28 © shutterstock, MitarArt, © Fotolia, Stephen Coburn, Monkey Business, © Alamy, Image Source, © Colourbox RF, © shutterstock, Andrey Armyagov, © Fotolia, Fotograv A. Gravante, © Fotolia, Galina Barskaya, © iStock, Brad Killer, S. 29 © shutterstock, Stephen Aaron Rees; S. 30 © Fotolia, Pumba; S. 31 © iStockphoto, Pumba1; S. 32 © Cornelsen Verlag, Lisa Lubin; S. 33 © Cornelsen Verlag, Lisa Lubin (6), © Cornelsen Verlag, Mark Wolters (2); S. 34 © shutterstock, Fotoksa, © Fotolia, © Fotolia, Anne Katrin Figge, Elvira Schäfer, © shutterstock, David Hughes, Chrislofoto, Phase4Photography, © iStockphoto, daniel rodriguez, © shutterstock, PHOTOCREO Michal Bednarek; © S. 35 © iStockphoto, ZoneCreative, Cliff Parnell, Neustockimages; S. 36 © shutterstock, Yarek Gora, © Alamy, Tetra Images, OJO Images, © shutterstock, Phase4Photography, © picture-alliance, John Gay/English Heritage.NMR/Mary Evans Picture Library, © Alamy, Westend61 GmbH, Catchlight Visual Services; S. 38 © iStockphoto, Valerijs Kostreckis, © Fotolia, 2happy, © shutterstock, Sashkin, © Fotolia, scphoto48, chickenstock, © iStockphoto, CostinT, © Fotolia, Kaarsten, c, © iStockphoto, PAVEL POSPISIL; S. 40 © Fotolia, Iosif Szasz-Fabian, Gudellaphoto, Rob Bouwman, luchshen, © shutterstock, Rafal Oikis, Philip Lange, © Pixelio, © shutterstock, hfng, © Fotolia, fuxart; S. 41 © Cornelsen Verlag, Lisa Lubin, © Courtesy of the Chicago Transport Authority; S. 43 © shutterstock, oliveromg, Alexander Chaikin, Mark Yuill, riekephotos, Andrejs Pidjass, Kurhan, Iakov Filimonov; S. 44 © iStockphoto, Mehmet Salih Guler, © shutterstock, MaszaS, © iStockphoto, ZoneCreative, HENG KONG CHEN, © Valerijs Kostreckis; S. 45 © Fotolia, Scott Griessel, © shutterstock, Johanna Goodyear, Tito Wong, © adpic, E. Wodicka, © Cornelsen Verlag, Mark Wolters, © shutterstock, c, Alexander Chaikin, © Colourbox RF; S. 46 © Cornelsen Verlag, Frank Maier; S. 47 © Cornelsen Verlag, Mark Wolters

Unser besonderer Dank gilt:
Bettina Kumpe, Lisa Lubin, Ulrich Gogolin und Mark Wolters